ROCKY POND BOOKS
An imprint of Penguin Random House LLC, New York

First published in the United States of America by Rocky Pond Books,
an imprint of Penguin Random House LLC, 2023
First paperback edition published 2024

Text copyright © 2023 by Mental Health America
Illustrations copyright © 2023 by Gemma Correll

Visit us online at PenguinRandomHouse.com.

Library of Congress Cataloging-in-Publication Data is available.

Printed in the United States of America

ISBN 9780593531419

1st Printing

LSCC

Design by Sylvia Bi • Text set in Sofia Pro

**With thanks to Shawn Goodman for his meaningful and wholehearted work
on this project**

This book is for anyone who has struggled and felt alone. It's for anyone who has felt unworthy. Or unloved. Or unlikeable. Or unsafe. This book is for anyone who has stared into the dark at 3:00 a.m., trying to stop the self-critical voice in their head. Trying to stop the questions.

Most importantly, this book is for anyone who has wondered if they can feel better and build a life without as much suffering.

**THIS BOOK IS FOR YOU!
YOU'RE IN THE RIGHT PLACE. KEEP READING.**

CONTENTS

HOW TO USE THIS BOOK

* There's no right or wrong way to read this book. Start anywhere you want, and don't feel the need to read straight through. There might be one section that's really important for you. It's okay to go there first.

* Read small chunks at a time, and give yourself a period afterward to think, or rest. It takes time to learn new information, so be patient with yourself.

* You may want to keep a journal as you read. If you do, write down your thoughts, feelings, and especially your questions.

* Skip and skim at will. Read out of order. Focus on the section that interests you the most, or targets the problem or question you're struggling with.

* This is not a how-to book with specific steps to follow. It's a guide, and the best guides are the ones you come back to at different times for different reasons. In other words, keep it on your shelf for later.

* Share it with people you care about, especially sections you think could help a friend or someone you trust to understand and support you better.

* Make this book your book. The margins are wide on purpose! Write notes or pictures in them. Highlight the parts that speak to you, or the ones you might want to revisit.

MENTAL ILLNESS FEELS LIKE...

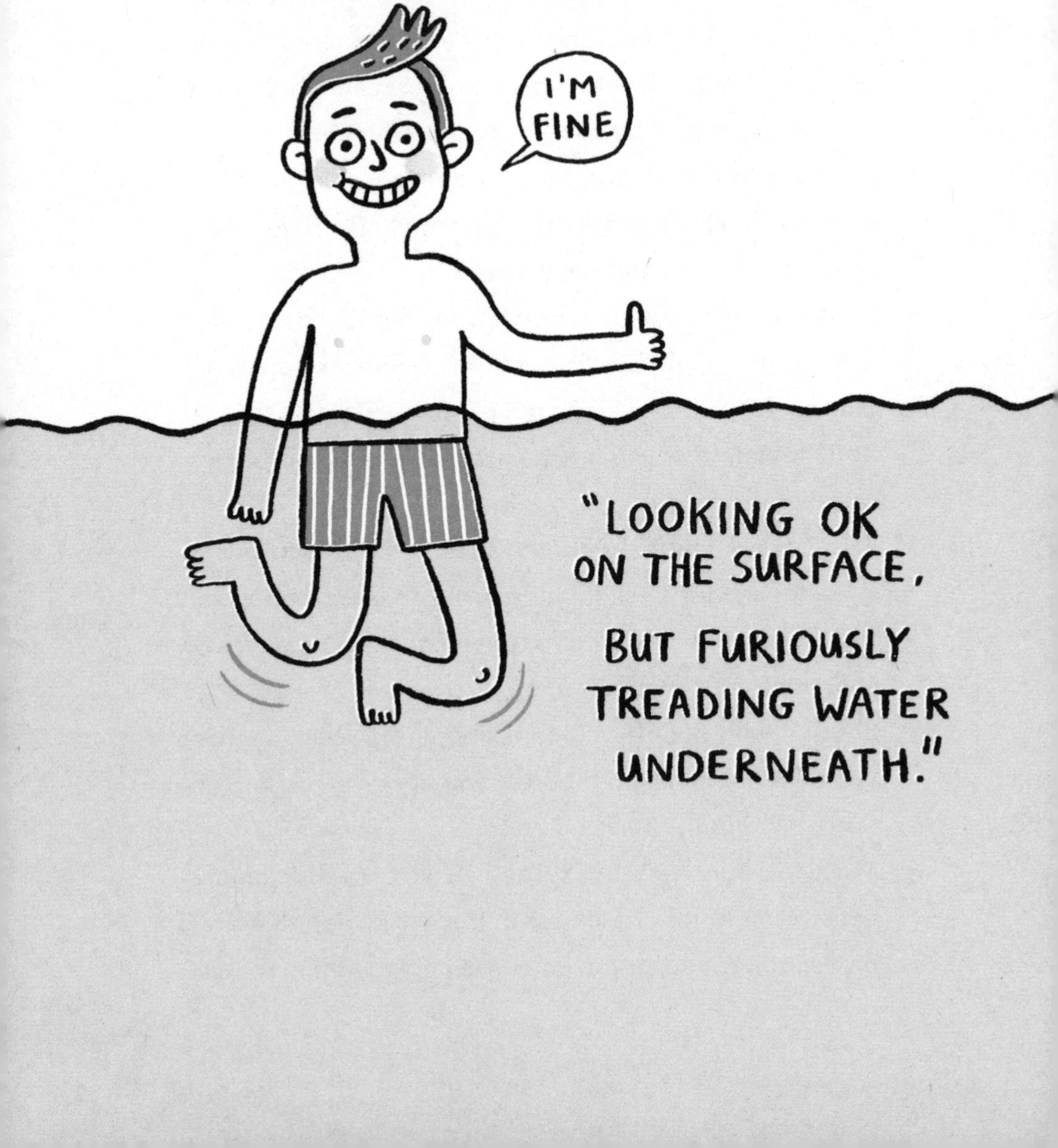

INTRODUCTION

DEAR READER,

Maybe it's too hard to believe right now that other people can understand what you're going through. And maybe it's even harder to believe that they can actually help. It's hard to trust, especially when others haven t earned your trust, or when you're feeling bad and don't know what to do. But if you've picked up this book, you already believe in the possibility that there's someone out there who can understand. There's someone out there who can help.

This book is made up of four parts. Each part answers a question. The first question is "Am I okay?" This part of the book will give you accurate information about the most common mental health problems. It's designed to tell you what you need to know in plain language, without mystery and confusion.

The second question is "How do we talk to one another about mental health?" This part of the book prepares you for having difficult conversations with the important people in your life. Having these kinds of conversations is a gateway to getting help. It's also a good way to lessen the loneliness and isolation that happens when you suffer in silence.

"How do I get professional help?" is the question answered in part three. Here you'll learn about different kinds of treatment and who is the right person to provide it. You'll learn all about therapy—how to find a good therapist and get the most from your sessions—medication, and hospitalization. And you'll learn about therapy apps, text lines, hotlines, and warmlines.

The last part of the book answers the question "How can I take better care of myself?" In this section, you'll learn general things like *managing difficult emotions* and *avoiding thinking traps*, and specific things like *what to do if you can't get out of bed* and *how to cope with a panic attack*.

A NOTE ON LANGUAGE

Words matter. Language matters. In this book you'll find plain language that affirms who you are as a unique person. You won't find a lot of psychological jargon, and you won't find research citations or clinical terms. There are plenty of other books that are written that way, and they have very different goals. The goals of this book are simple: to give you good information on how to start taking care of your mental health, and to empower you to take the first steps on your journey to feeling better.

Throughout this book we will use person-centered language. Person-centered language places the whole person above any illness, disability, or label. We will say a person living with schizophrenia, rather than a schizophrenic. We will say a person living with a substance use disorder, rather than an addict. Person-centered language values the dignity and uniqueness of all people. And most importantly, it discourages thinking that a person's disability or condition is a characteristic of their identity.

A NOTE ON BEGINNINGS

Reading this book means you are taking a step toward healing. You are starting the journey from isolation to connectedness, from feeling lost and hopeless to the beginnings of self-confidence and stability. The journey may be long and difficult. You may need to work through painful emotions and learn new skills. At times, you may feel like the work is too intense, too challenging. But you can do this! And remember: Positive changes happen when we speak honestly about what we are feeling and what kind of support we need. The journey is worth it. *You* are worth it!

PART ONE

AM I OKAY?

MENTAL ILLNESS FEELS LIKE...

"CONSTANTLY CHASING
A 'NORMAL' LIFE."

Signs and Symptoms of Mental Health Problems

For a moment, try to think about your mental health the way you think about your physical health. We all have good days and bad days, and ups and downs in our physical health. This is totally normal. Some days you might feel a little tired, sore, or under the weather. That doesn't necessarily mean you're sick. You know you're physically sick when you notice that something has changed for the worse—you were feeling fine, but today you have a high temperature and you've lost your voice. Something prevents you from functioning properly. Things that are normally easy now feel a lot more difficult. Maybe it's even bad enough that you can't make it to school or work.

Mental health problems are similar. Good days and bad days. Ups and downs. The difference is that instead of looking for physical symptoms, like a runny nose or an upset stomach, you're looking at your thoughts, feelings, and behaviors. Here are some examples of things that might tip you off:

* You used to be really cheerful and outgoing, but lately all you want to do is sit in your room.
* Things you used to enjoy have lost their appeal. Food doesn't taste as good as it used to, and all your favorite music sounds boring.
* You're falling asleep in class or at work. It's hard to pay attention, study, and keep track of your assignments.
* Your friend is talking and you're trying hard to listen, but you can't concentrate. All you can think about are bad things that might happen to you.
* You're having thoughts of death, or of hurting yourself, or of killing yourself.
* You can't leave the house without organizing and aligning your shoes and clothes. You do this so much that it's making you late for school.
* You're always irritated, and you can't stop snapping at people.
* Recently you started hearing voices that no one else seems to hear.

Maybe just one of these applies to you. Or none of them. The important thing is to notice any change in your thoughts, feelings, or behaviors that makes it harder for you to go about your daily life.

GETTING BETTER

Before we go any further, it's important to remember that no matter what kind of mental health problem someone is facing, it is always possible to get better. Don't forget this! Finding help is important. Connecting with others is important. So is being kind to yourself and trying not to judge yourself too harshly.

DO I NEED TO PUT A LABEL ON IT?

Let's talk about labels, or what to call the different kinds of mental health problems.

The label a mental health professional uses to talk about a specific mental health condition is called a diagnosis. An example of a diagnosis might be "generalized anxiety disorder" or "bipolar disorder." There are a lot of diagnoses that describe different mental health conditions—they go way beyond just "depression." Some people feel comforted to know that there's a name for what they've been experiencing. Other people don't like it; they might feel that the diagnosis is too medical and doesn't leave room for who they really are as a person. Both views are okay, and you can decide for yourself where you stand.

This part of the book discusses the symptoms of the most common mental health conditions, but keep this in mind: You don't need a diagnosis to get help. Some therapists actually prefer not to diagnose their clients. And even people without a diagnosis or even a serious mental health problem can benefit from therapy. But for many people it can be helpful to have a name for what you're going through. Labels are there to help you, not limit you or keep you in a box. With the right diagnosis it can be easier to find helpful information online, to get the right kind of treatment, and to connect with other people who have had similar experiences.

SO HOW DO I FIND OUT WHAT I HAVE?

Sometimes people can get a good sense of what condition they might have from reading about it online and talking to people who have had similar experiences. But it's easy to get carried away. Ever use WebMD to check your physical symptoms and come away thinking you must have some rare disease? Mental health conditions can be the same way.

A good starting point is to take a mental health screening test, and we've included one at the end of this chapter. You can use your results to start a conversation with your friends and family, and to monitor your progress over time.

Eventually, if you want to be officially diagnosed, you'll need to meet with a doctor or therapist. They'll ask you questions and use their training and experience to determine whether your symptoms meet the criteria for a specific diagnosis. If you want to do this, try to meet with someone who specializes in mental health, like a psychiatrist, psychologist, or a therapist. Your regular family doctor can diagnose common conditions such as depression, anxiety, and ADHD and can refer you to a specialist if they think it's needed.

Keep in mind that even mental health professionals aren't perfect. If you've been diagnosed and you don't think it's accurate, it may be a good idea to get a second opinion. And remember: A diagnosis doesn't define you—it's just a way of connecting you with more specific help.

Mood Disorders

DEPRESSION

Feeling sad is a normal human experience, but feeling sad too much of the time can cause distress and major life problems. You might withdraw from your family and friends, have a hard time in school or work, or feel overwhelmed by activities. When too much sadness affects your life, you might have depression.

Depression is a type of mood disorder. Mood disorders occur when changes in mood go way beyond the normal ups and downs of everyday life. Episodes of depression last at least two weeks at a time, but sometimes they can last for months or even years.

One of the difficulties in talking about depression is that it shows up differently from person to person. When you read through the following content, you'll see that one person with depression may sleep too much, while another may sleep too little. Don't let this confuse or overwhelm you. It just means that everyone is different, and mental health conditions are caused by many different factors. Thus, they can present differently.

DEPRESSION FEELS LIKE...

"A TERRIBLE SINKING SENSATION."

Many people make the mistake of thinking that depression is a choice, or an expression of someone's personality. While making good healthy choices is important, there are many other factors that determine whether or not someone develops depression, such as genetics, trauma, medications, or medical conditions. It can be difficult to pinpoint the cause of depression because sometimes it's not just one thing that is triggering your mood. Depression can affect anyone. Regardless of your life circumstances, if you think you might be depressed, the sooner you seek help, the better off you'll be in managing it. You may feel undeserving of the help or that other people are worse off than you, but that's flat-out incorrect. You totally deserve to get help and feel better.

HOW DO I KNOW IF I'M SAD OR DEPRESSED?

Depression is about being sad, but it's much more than that. Depression involves a lot of other symptoms, like feeling exhausted much of the time, losing interest in activities you normally enjoy, or thoughts of death and suicide. Episodes of depression last at least two weeks at a time. They can be triggered by a sad or disruptive event or they can come out of nowhere.

Sadness, on the other hand, even extreme sadness, can be a normal reaction to things like a breakup or losing a loved one. That said, regular sadness can turn into depression. If the feelings don't get better over time, or if your mood starts to get in the way of your daily life, you might be developing a case of depression.

DEPRESSION FEELS LIKE...

"THIS."

MISSING

MY MOTIVATION TO DO STUFF

Physical changes can also affect your mood and look like depression—things like hormone changes due to puberty or certain medical treatments or conditions. Drug and alcohol use can also change your mood. Some people try using drugs and alcohol to self-medicate underlying depression or another mental illness. This is never a good idea. Talk to your doctor if any of these apply to you.

Here's a list of the most common symptoms of depression. You don't have to experience all of these to be depressed. Everyone's experience of depression is slightly different.

* Feeling low, empty inside, or irritable most of the day every day
* Losing interest in activities you normally enjoy
* Changes in appetite or weight. This could go in either direction: eating too much and gaining weight, or not eating enough and losing weight.
* Changes in sleep—either not being able to sleep or sleeping too much
* Changes in activity—feeling restless inside or feeling sluggish
* Feeling exhausted even when you seem to be getting enough sleep
* Speaking or moving slowly, fidgeting, or pacing

* Feelings of worthlessness or guilt
* Difficulty thinking, concentrating, or making decisions
* Thoughts of death or suicide

WHAT IF I'VE BEEN THINKING ABOUT DEATH?

It's normal to think about death at different times in your life. People living with depression may think about death often. Sometimes this involves thinking about suicide, but not always. Many people living with depression think about not existing, or wonder if the world would be better without them. If you are having suicidal thoughts or are planning to complete suicide, stop reading and reach out to get help now. **Call the National Suicide Prevention Lifeline at 988, or text MHA to 741741** to be connected with a trained crisis counselor from **Crisis Text Line.** An alternative is to call a warmline. If you want to read more about suicidal thoughts and learn how to stay safe, go to page 139.

BIPOLAR DISORDER

People with bipolar disorder experience extended periods of extreme high energy and mood called mania, and extended periods of extreme low energy and mood called depression. These episodes can vary in length, but they normally last from a few weeks to several months. In between, there are periods where you feel "normal."

While everyone has ups and downs in mood and energy, with bipolar disorder the shifts are much more severe. Even so, it can be difficult to tell the difference between bipolar disorder and normal mood swings. Many people have mood swings, but when these feelings persist and get in the way of your relationships and your ability to function in school and other parts of your life, bipolar disorder could be the cause. Let's talk a little more about what manic and depressive episodes look like.

BIPOLAR DISORDER FEELS LIKE...

"MOOD SWINGS."

MANIA

During a manic episode, you might experience some of the following:

* Having lots of energy
* Feeling unstoppable
* Racing thoughts
* Not sleeping
* Impulsive behavior, like spending too much money, having risky sex, or abusing drugs and alcohol
* Psychotic symptoms like paranoia or seeing or hearing things that other people don't
* Exaggerated sense of self-importance and preoccupation with fantasies of unlimited success, power, superiority, or ideal love

You may have noticed that some of these symptoms sound like fun, while others sound pretty scary. Many people feel great during manic episodes—but often make poor decisions that they regret later. During a really serious manic episode, some people are hospitalized for suicidal behavior or extreme symptoms that can be dangerous.

Hypomania is a less intense form of mania. The symptoms

are similar, but milder. The impact on people's daily lives isn't as severe.

One last thing about manic symptoms: They are big changes from what a person is typically like. If you *always* speak quickly, make impulsive decisions, and don't sleep much, those aren't signs of a manic episode.

DEPRESSION

During a depressive episode, you might experience some of the following:

* Feeling sad
* Feeling worthless, numb, or empty
* Low energy
* Changes in sleep and eating habits
* Thoughts of death or suicide

OTHER ASPECTS OF BIPOLAR DISORDER

Like other mental illnesses, bipolar disorder doesn't have a single cause. Instead, it has a variety of risk factors like genetics, environment, childhood trauma, stressful events, unhealthy habits, drug and alcohol use, and brain chemistry. It is often the interaction between these risk factors that determines whether a person will develop bipolar disorder. For example, if bipolar disorder runs in a person's family, they live in a stressful environment, and are using drugs and alcohol, they may be more likely to experience symptoms.

In bipolar disorder, periods of mania and depression usually last weeks or even months. When someone experiences four or more of these episodes within a single year, this is called "rapid cycling." It's also possible to experience mania and depression at the same time. This is called a "mixed episode."

Being diagnosed with bipolar disorder can feel scary, but it is treatable, and recovery is possible. With a combination of therapy, lifestyle changes, support, and/or medication, you can live a full, meaningful life. There are many people who live with bipolar disorder who are successful and have made great contributions to the world.

Anxiety Disorders

Anxiety is what you feel when you're worried about something. There's both a physical and a mental component. Your body tenses up, and your mind becomes fixated on the thing you're worried about. It can be hard to concentrate on anything else. Anxiety can also affect your appetite and make it hard to sleep.

It's normal to experience anxiety from time to time. A little anxiety can be useful. For example, if you're anxious about an upcoming exam or work assignment, it might motivate you to study, focus on the task, and feel more prepared. But anxiety can get out of hand. If you're so anxious that you can't concentrate, the anxiety is no longer useful. And if you're worried about things that aren't likely to happen, or things that are beyond your control? That can really affect the quality of your life.

ANXIETY FEELS LIKE...

HOW DO I KNOW IF I HAVE AN ANXIETY DISORDER OR "JUST STRESS"?

If you are having these concerns, you are not alone. Anxiety disorders are common and manageable.

SYMPTOMS OF AN ANXIETY DISORDER

Everyone's experience with anxiety is different, but in general the symptoms cause serious problems in their lives. Difficulty concentrating is common and can make it hard to do well in school or at a job. Many people take extreme measures to avoid situations that might trigger their anxiety. They might isolate themselves from others, avoid public spaces, or change their daily routines to avoid something that makes them anxious.

Common symptoms of anxiety disorders include:

* Feeling restless and irritable
* Difficulty concentrating

27

* Muscle pain, tightness, or soreness
* Trouble falling asleep or staying asleep
* Feeling exhausted even after a full night's sleep
* Going out of your way to avoid situations that make you anxious
* Intrusive thoughts (unwanted thoughts or worries that won't go away)
* Panic attacks (see page 32)

DIFFERENT TYPES OF ANXIETY DISORDERS

GENERALIZED ANXIETY DISORDER

This is the most common anxiety disorder and is probably what most people think about when they hear the term "anxiety disorder." People with generalized anxiety disorder tend to feel frightened, distressed, and uneasy for no apparent reason or in ways that are not proportional to their circumstances. Their excessive worry lasts for at least six months, and is focused on a number of different events or activities (like taking tests *and* having to talk about yourself in a job interview).

GENERALIZED ANXIETY DISORDER FEELS LIKE...

"THE MOMENT THE ROLLER COASTER STOPS, RIGHT BEFORE THE DROP—

BUT ALL THE TIME."

SOCIAL ANXIETY DISORDER

This is another common anxiety disorder and is characterized by extreme fear or anxiety in social settings. It's more than being shy or an introvert. With social anxiety disorder, there is an intense fear of social situations in which you might do or say the wrong thing and then be exposed to judgment or criticism by others. Just the thought of going to a party or even having a one-on-one conversation with a new person can result in increased heart rate, sweating, and racing thoughts.

It's common for people with social anxiety to isolate and feel very alone, making recovery harder. While most people have concerns about acceptance and embarrassment, the extreme anxiety and dread that accompany social anxiety disorder are so overwhelming that a person may find it hard to function in daily life and may avoid the anxiety-inducing situations altogether.

PHOBIAS

A phobia is when you are extremely afraid or anxious about a specific situation. While it's normal to be afraid of snakes, spiders, or clowns, when it's a phobia, the reaction

is out of proportion to the actual situation. It's so distressing that you may go out of your way to avoid the situation. Other common phobias include fear of heights, fear of open or crowded spaces, and fear of blood or needles.

PANIC DISORDER

People with panic disorder experience panic attacks, which are periods of intense fear and discomfort. The symptoms are different for everyone but often involve trouble breathing, feeling like you're going to pass out or even die, and feeling detached from your surroundings. People often think they're having a heart attack. Panic attacks can be scary, to the point where the person experiencing them becomes fearful of having another.

The important thing to remember is that panic attacks usually won't last longer than ten minutes, they aren't life threatening, and they can be treated. During a panic attack, your body is in "fight-or-flight" mode, reacting to a threat that isn't there or one that doesn't need such an extreme reaction. It can happen unexpectedly, even when you feel at ease. If you have panic attacks, you can learn and practice a few skills like self-talk (see page 127) and deep breathing.

PANIC DISORDER FEELS LIKE...

"THERE'S AN ELEPHANT SITTING ON MY CHEST."

OBSESSIVE-COMPULSIVE DISORDER

Obsessive-Compulsive Disorder, or OCD, is when a person has repeated, unwanted thoughts and behaviors, such as feeling the need to excessively wash their hands or repeatedly check locks. If you happen to like everything neat and in order, you're not "sooo OCD" (and people with OCD would like you to stop saying that). OCD is characterized by obsessions and/or compulsions. These are very serious intrusive thoughts and behaviors that are disruptive to your life.

OCD FEELS LIKE...

"A DAILY BATTLE WITH MY OWN BRAIN."

DISORDERS OF ATTENTION

ATTENTION DEFICIT
HYPERACTIVITY DISORDER (ADHD)

ADHD is one of the most common mental health conditions among young adults. There are three types of ADHD: inattentive, hyperactive (or impulsive), and combined. It is often first noticed in school but can be diagnosed in college and adulthood. To be diagnosed with ADHD, you must show symptoms in at least two settings, such as home and school, and the symptoms must be present for at least six months. Specialists have agreed that you must have at least six symptoms from the following lists for an accurate diagnosis.

INATTENTIVE BEHAVIOR

Symptoms include:

* Difficulty following instructions
* Difficulty focusing on tasks
* Losing things at school and at home

* Forgetfulness
* Having trouble keeping track of schedule and school work
* Being easily distracted or having difficulty listening
* Lack of attention to detail, disorganization, or making careless mistakes
* Failure to complete homework or tasks

HYPERACTIVE BEHAVIOR

Symptoms include:

* Being always on the go
* Fidgeting
* Talking excessively
* Interrupting
* Risk-taking behavior
* Frustration when required to "sit around"

Many young adults have some symptoms, but not enough for a diagnosis. Just because you have a lot of energy or have difficulty paying attention in school does not mean you have ADHD. An accurate diagnosis relies on the presence of a range of symptoms and difficulties that prevent you from performing at an appropriate level for your age and intelligence.

ADHD FEELS LIKE...

"THERE ARE TOO MANY TABS OPEN IN MY HEAD."

Trauma and Post-Traumatic Stress Disorder

We often think about trauma and PTSD as something military veterans experience, but it can happen to anyone. If you have seen or experienced something that really shocked or scared you, or threatened your sense of safety, you may be dealing with trauma. Anything that is highly stressful to you can be traumatic.

Trauma is different for everyone. It can be a one-time event or ongoing, such as discrimination or childhood neglect. What seems normal to someone else might be traumatic for you. A traumatic experience can be a threat to your physical safety, such as a car accident or an assault. It could also be something emotional or social, such as online bullying. School-related trauma (like bullying or unfair punishment) often leads to school avoidance, which is when the thought of going to school makes you anxious and afraid. BIPOC students (Black, indigenous, and people of color) are vulnerable to racial trauma due to living in a system of white supremacy.

Race-based discrimination and violence have been prominent in media coverage, which can be triggering and retraumatizing for students with marginalized identities.

WHAT'S IT LIKE TO GO THROUGH TRAUMA?

Most people feel anxious and afraid during and after a traumatic event. Some develop long-term symptoms that impact their day-to-day functioning. Trauma can occur at any age, but it has a particularly long-lasting impact when it occurs in childhood or adolescence, when the brain is still developing rapidly.

We all respond to situations and feelings differently, so not everyone who shares an experience with you will have the same reaction. There is no "right" or "wrong" way to think, feel, or act after experiencing a traumatic event. But you may find yourself experiencing some of these symptoms:

Common Emotional Symptoms of Trauma

* Fear, anxiety
* Shock, disbelief
* Confusion, difficulty focusing
* Anger or irritability
* Guilt, shame
* Alienation from peers
* Sadness, hopelessness
* Feeling disconnected or numb
* Feeling like everything is out of your control

Common Physical Symptoms

* Exaggerated startle response
* Trouble sleeping, nightmares
* Fatigue, exhaustion
* Dizziness, shakiness
* Racing heart, fast breathing
* Feeling on edge
* Body aches/pains, muscle tension
* Frequent headaches or stomachaches
* Increased substance use and other risky behavior

PTSD FEELS LIKE...

"A NEVER-ENDING TIGHTROPE BETWEEN FIGHT AND FLIGHT."

HOW LONG DO THE EFFECTS OF TRAUMA LAST?

Trauma symptoms typically last from a few days to a few months. You may not feel like your normal self for a while. In many cases, symptoms will gradually fade as time passes and as you process what happened. Once you're feeling better, it's common for painful memories or emotions to resurface occasionally—especially in response to event anniversaries, or other things that remind you of the trauma. Things that bring back memories or symptoms of trauma are called triggers.

WILL I EVER FEEL BETTER?

Be patient with yourself! Trauma is hard to deal with—but that doesn't mean that you'll never be okay again. There are a lot of ways for people with trauma to cope with their symptoms and improve their quality of life. Many people who have experienced trauma live fulfilling lives with the help of their support system, therapy, lifestyle changes, and/or medication.

Some people experience traumatic events without developing a mental illness. The level of support someone has during and after a traumatic event can influence how they cope and the likelihood of developing a mental health condition. If a person lacks supports or the trauma is unusually intense—or maybe it's not overly intense but it continues over time—they can develop serious symptoms that cause a lot of emotional pain and can make it hard to function. If you develop enough of these symptoms, you might have what's called Post-Traumatic Stress Disorder (PTSD). Let's learn exactly what that means.

The telltale signs of PTSD:

* **Repeatedly thinking about the trauma.** You may find that thoughts about the trauma come to mind even when you don't want them to. You might also have nightmares or flashbacks.
* **Being constantly alert or on guard.** You may be easily startled or angered, irritable or anxious and preoccupied with staying safe. You might become hyper-aware of your surroundings and see danger everywhere.
* **Avoiding reminders of the trauma.** You may not want to talk about the event or be around people or places that remind you of the event. You may even forget details about the event or suppress your memories.

* Intense negative emotions and beliefs. You may feel depressed, anxious, guilty, or angry. You might blame yourself for the trauma, or believe that no one can be trusted and that the world is a dangerous place.

Other symptoms may include:

* Feeling emotionally numb
* Trouble concentrating or sleeping
* Losing interest in activities you normally enjoy
* Relationship problems: having trouble with intimacy, or feeling detached from your family and friends
* Physical symptoms: chronic pain, headaches, stomach pain, diarrhea or constipation, tightness or burning in the chest, muscle cramps, or lower back pain
* Panic attacks: a sudden feeling of intense fear (which may seem totally unrelated to the event), with shortness of breath, dizziness, sweating, nausea, and racing heart
* Substance use problems: using drugs or alcohol to cope with, or forget, the emotional pain
* Other mental health conditions such as anxiety, depression, or suicidal thoughts

Eating Disorders

EATING DISORDERS FEEL LIKE...

"I'M IN A HALL OF MIRRORS
AND I CAN'T TELL WHICH
ONE IS THE 'REAL' ME."

Eating disorders are mental health conditions that involve unhealthy behaviors, obsessions, and compulsions around food, exercise, and/or body shape. They affect people of all ages, races, backgrounds, socioeconomic statuses, religions, genders, and sexual orientations. They are the most lethal of any mental health conditions and can have serious consequences, including bone damage, hair loss, muscle loss, rupture of the stomach, and diabetes.

Most people think of eating disorders as an obsession with being skinny, but they are far more complicated than that and are thought to result from a combination of biological, psychological, and social factors. Many people with eating disorders have other mental health conditions, including depression, anxiety, PTSD, and addiction. Trauma, especially sexual trauma, is very common among individuals with eating disorders.

It's confusing for many people to tell the difference between healthy and unhealthy eating. One reason for this is because American culture promotes excessive dieting. Many people with eating disorders resist getting help because they think they're "not sick enough." But early treatment is important, so remember: There's no specific body weight or level of severity that you must reach before you deserve help or support.

While eating disorders are complicated, people do recover from them. The earlier you get help the better, both for psychological and physical recovery. With services and supports that can include a therapist, dietician, psychiatrist, peers, support groups, and/or a primary care physician, people can and do go on to have healthy relationships with food and exercise.

The most common types of eating disorders are:

* ANOREXIA. Anorexia involves restricting food intake, significant weight loss, intense fear of weight gain, and a distorted perception of appearance. A person with anorexia often has very specific rules and rituals around food and tends to socially isolate.
* BINGE EATING DISORDER. Binge eating disorder is when a person repeatedly eats abnormally large amounts of food in short time frames. It's different from overeating in that it causes serious pain and shame, and the person often feels out of control.
* BULIMIA. Bulimia involves both bingeing and purging. Purging means vomiting to eliminate the food that was eaten, laxative or drug use, fasting, or over-exercising.

* AVOIDANT/RESTRICTIVE FOOD INTAKE DISORDER (ARFID). **ARFID is** when a person limits the amount and/or types of food consumed; but unlike anorexia, it's not because of distress about body shape or size or weight.
* OTHER SPECIFIED FEEDING OR EATING DISORDER (OSFED). **This is** the term used when someone has eating disorder behaviors that don't meet the guidelines for other eating disorders. For example, a person restricts food intake, has an intense fear of gaining weight, and a distorted perception of their appearance, but they haven't lost enough weight to be classified as underweight by their doctor, which means they do not meet the full criteria for anorexia despite having all the other signs.

WHY IS IT SO HARD TO RECOVER?

Eating disorders often develop slowly. You may not realize what is happening until you are seriously struggling physically, emotionally, and psychologically. People around you may not notice, either. Some may even compliment you for eating healthier or losing weight, which sends a very confusing message.

Another reason why recovery is so hard is because the people around you may dismiss your issues, especially when you don't look the way people think eating disorders "should look." You may even dismiss them yourself. This can make it hard to ask for help or to stay in treatment. Remember: You don't have to look a certain way to be deserving of help and support.

Lastly, not all mental health professionals will understand what you're going through.

It is important to find the right team, such as a psychiatrist, psychologist, nutritionist, and a support network of friends and family, to help you focus on how to recover and stay well.

Psychosis

PSYCHOSIS FEELS LIKE...

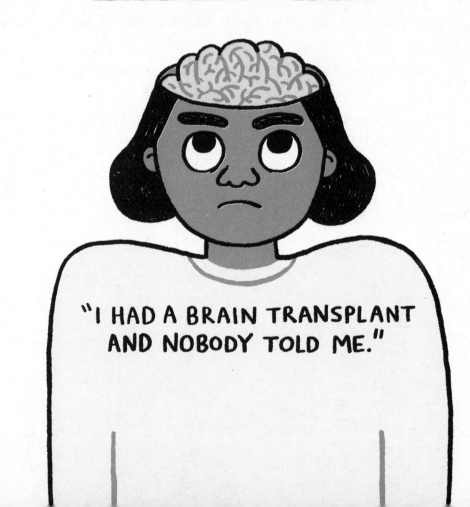

Psychosis is a symptom, not a specific type of mental illness. People most commonly think of it as a symptom of schizophrenia, but it can also show up in bipolar disorder during a manic episode, or in other circumstances. There's even such a thing as psychotic depression. Some medications or recreational drugs can also trigger psychosis, as can extreme stress or going for a long time without sleep.

Psychosis is when a person loses contact with reality. It becomes hard to tell what's real and what isn't. The symptoms can be mild or extreme, and psychosis can show up in many different ways:

Thoughts:

* Believing you are being watched, or that other people can read your mind
* Paranoia or bizarre fears that won't go away
* Feeling like things aren't real or quite right
* Trouble focusing and remembering things
* Feeling disconnected or numb about important situations
* Extreme fear for no apparent reason

Perceptions:

✳ Hearing sounds or voices that others don't
✳ Seeing ghost-like shadows or wavy lines
✳ Suddenly having a decreased sense of smell
✳ Becoming very sensitive to light, sound, or touch

Behaviors:

✳ Neglecting personal hygiene
✳ Nonsensical or bizarre speech or writing
✳ Withdrawing from family and friends
✳ Anger or fear toward loved ones
✳ Changes in sleep, including reversal: sleeping during the day and staying awake at night
✳ Changes in appetite
✳ Suddenly being unable to function at school or work
✳ Behaviors that are strange or don't seem like "you"

Psychosis tends to get worse over time, so it's important to start seeking treatment as early as possible. Experiencing psychosis can be scary and confusing, and friends and family may not know what to do. The good news is that recovery is possible. Whether after a single experience or when symptoms occur throughout one's life, a person who experiences psychosis can live fully and meaningfully and contribute to their community. It's important to get help as soon as possible, though.

Signs and Symptoms That You Shouldn't Ignore:

* Thoughts or plans of hurting or killing yourself or another person
* Hearing voices or seeing things that no one else can hear or see
* Unexplainable changes in thinking, speech, or writing
* Being overly suspicious or fearful
* A serious drop in school performance
* Sudden personality changes that are bizarre or out of character

Mental Health Assessment

Online screening is one of the quickest and easiest ways to determine whether you are experiencing symptoms of a mental health condition. This scientifically validated questionnaire can be used to see if you are having emotional, attentional, or behavioral difficulties.

These results are not meant to be a diagnosis. You can meet with a doctor or therapist to get a diagnosis and/or access therapy or medication. Sharing these results with someone you trust can be a great place to start. And if you are interested in completing this screening or others online, visit mhascreening.org to access more information and resources.

For each item please mark how often you:

	NEVER	SOMETIMES	OFTEN
1. Complain of aches or pains			
2. Spend more time alone			
3. Tire easily, little energy			
4. Fidgety, unable to sit still			
5. Have trouble with teacher			
6. Less interested in school			
7. Act as if driven by motor			
8. Daydream too much			
9. Distract easily			
10. Are afraid of new situations			
11. Feel sad, unhappy			
12. Are irritable, angry			

	NEVER	SOMETIMES	OFTEN
13. Feel hopeless			
14. Have trouble concentrating			
15. Less interested in friends			
16. Fight with other children			
17. Absent from school			
18. School grades dropping			
19. Down on yourself			
20. Visit doctor, finding nothing wrong			
21. Have trouble sleeping			
22. Worry a lot			
23. Want to be with parent more than before			
24. Feel that you are bad			

	NEVER	SOMETIMES	OFTEN
25. Take unnecessary risks			
26. Get hurt frequently			
27. Seem to be having less fun			
28. Act younger than children your age			
29. Do not listen to rules			
30. Do not show feelings			
31. Do not understand other people's feelings			
32. Tease others			
33. Blame others for your troubles			
34. Take things that do not belong to you			
35. Refuse to share			

Scoring:

* "NEVER" = 0, "SOMETIMES" = 1, and "OFTEN" = 2
* The total score is calculated by adding together the score for each of the 35 items.
* For people ages 6 through 16, a cutoff score of 28 or higher indicates psychological impairment. Items that are left blank are simply ignored (i.e., score equals 0). If four or more items are left blank, the questionnaire is considered invalid.
* A score of 28 or higher suggests the need for further evaluation by a qualified health or mental health professional.

PART TWO

TALKING ABOUT MENTAL HEALTH

I'M HERE FOR YOU
AND I'M NOT GOING ANYWHERE
EXCEPT MAYBE TO THE STORE TO BUY ICE CREAM, BUT I PROMISE TO COME RIGHT BACK AND SHARE IT WITH YOU!

Let's say you've been feeling depressed or anxious. You haven't been sleeping well, and it's harder to focus in school and get your work done. This has been going on for a few weeks, and people are starting to notice. You've thought about talking to someone, but it's just too scary. What if you open up to them and they look at you differently? What if they don't understand or, worse, they say something mean or critical?

Now imagine the same scenario, but you ask a person you trust to give you an hour without interruptions so you can talk. It could be a parent, sibling, friend, or someone else who makes you feel safe and is a good listener. You tell this person what you've been going through. And, after listening attentively, and asking a few questions, this is what the person says:

I'm so glad you trusted me. Thank you for telling me.

I want to help. How can I help?

I'm sorry you've been going through this alone. It must have been tough. But now you don't have to bear it alone anymore.

It would be so reassuring to hear these words, wouldn't it? Yet so many of us suffer through our problems alone, typically because of fear and shame. But you'd be surprised how many people you know have also dealt with—or are dealing with—depression, anxiety, trouble paying attention, eating disorders, trauma, and other mental health problems. And if they haven't been dealing with it themselves, someone in their family or circle of friends has. While not everyone will understand, many people will.

No matter what path you choose, it's important to reach out to someone to get help. Whether it's someone you already know or a professional resource such as a therapist, support group, text line, hotline, or warmline, getting it out and acknowledging how you're feeling is a massive first step. (You'll find more information about these resources in Part Three and the Resources section.)

If you're worried about what to say, this book can help you prepare for this conversation. Finding the right language to describe your experience can make all the difference. Remember, you don't have to tell everyone in your life, but it's really important to tell *someone*. You do not have to deal with this alone.

And if you're worried about other people's reactions,

keep in mind that hurtful comments often stem from someone being poorly informed and fearful. Negative media images and a popular culture that lacks respect for people living with mental health conditions make it worse. One antidote is to learn how to talk about mental health. It's natural to avoid difficult conversations, but engaging in them—as hard as that can be—can lead to greater understanding and self-respect, and less suffering.

Prepping to Talk to Others About Mental Health

MENTAL ILLNESS FEELS LIKE...

Chances are, you're reading this book because you already know you need to talk to someone and get help. But doubts are common. In fact, they're pretty normal. If you've thought about it and you're still not sure, here are a few reasons to seek someone out:

* Your thoughts or actions seem out of sync with how other people think and behave.
* Your thoughts, feelings, or behaviors are starting to impact your life at home, at school, or with friends.
* You've had some of these signs and symptoms for more than a week:
  o Feeling sad, empty, or hopeless
  o Feeling overly worried
  o Irritability or restlessness
  o Not being able to do schoolwork
  o Loss of appetite or eating too much
  o Problems with concentration, memory, or thinking
  o Loss of interest in things you used to enjoy
  o Withdrawal from others
  o Feeling bad or worthless
  o Changes in sleep patterns or energy levels
  o Thinking about hurting or killing yourself

- Sensitivity to sound, sight, smell, or touch
- Feeling like your brain is playing tricks on you

WHO SHOULD I TALK TO?

Take a moment to think about who you might feel comfortable talking to about your mental health. Someone you trust. Someone who will listen to you and help you plan your next steps. Someone who will not spread rumors or gossip after the conversation. Thinking about what you need from this person can help decide who to go to. Do you need someone who is going to give advice or do you need someone who will just listen and be there? Maybe it's someone you can cry with. While this could be a family member (parent, grandparent, aunt, uncle, sibling), you can also seek out a person at your school or college (nurse, guidance counselor, or social worker), or in your congregation (rabbi, pastor, imam, youth group leader), or community (coach, neighbor).

Ideally, the person should be kind, and a good listener. It might surprise you how many people are willing to listen and want to understand. There will be some who just won't get it, and it's not your job to make them understand—just keep trying to find the right support system for you: someone who listens to you with openness and helps you feel less alone, less isolated.

If you can't think of anyone you feel ready to talk to, try a stranger: There are many great hotlines, warmlines, text lines, and online support groups run by trained volunteers or employees whose job it is to listen to those who reach out (see Resources at the end of the book). Talking to a stranger can help you feel safer about what you're sharing, and strangers may be able to offer more objective feedback than the people involved in your life.

Here's a list of some of the people you might ask to talk to. Jot ideas here and start with whoever feels most comfortable for you right now. You can always open up to more people later on.

* Parent or guardian
* Friend
* Sibling
* Teacher
* Doctor or therapist
* Coach or club leader

* Aunt or uncle
* School nurse, social worker, or school psychologist
* School guidance counselor
* Neighbor
* Cousin
* Grandparent
* Youth group leader
* Religious leader
* A friend's parent
* Support group
* Anonymous help line

WHAT SHOULD I EXPECT WHEN I START THE CONVERSATION?

You've made the decision to talk with someone about your mental health, and you even know who. Now what? You're probably nervous about how things will go. Maybe the person won't understand or won't know what to do. Maybe you'll get emotional and have trouble speaking. It's okay. It doesn't have to be perfect, and if you're really worried about this, you can try writing your thoughts down first.

This can help you get your words in order so you know how to express yourself. You can even write a letter to the person, or a long text, or a series of texts. If you're unsure of how to write a letter or what to put in it, use the sample at the end of this chapter. All you have to do is fill in the blanks.

Here are a few typical first-conversation experiences that you can anticipate:

INTERRUPTIONS

It's a fact: People interrupt. Phones ping and buzz. Attention spans are short. There are a few things you can do to set the stage for a good conversation that minimizes this risk. First, make sure it's the right time to talk. This means both you and the person you're talking to have an open window of time, and neither will have to cut the conversation short to check a phone or take care of other obligations. Plan to set aside at least thirty minutes to an hour. Second, you can set a good example for the other person by silencing your phone and putting it away—or at least turning it screen-down. Third, you can set an expectation by starting out with something like, "Thanks for talking to me now and giving me your attention. I really appreciate it."

AWKWARDNESS

Having a serious talk about your mental health might be a little awkward at first. For a lot of people, talking about anything related to their health or body can be kind of tough. Talking about emotions and relationships can be even tougher. Expect a certain amount of discomfort, and silences. It's okay. Accept it—maybe even mention it—and move through it.

RELIEF

At some point in the conversation, you'll probably feel relieved. If you've been keeping something to yourself for a long time, sharing can feel like a weight has been lifted. And it's not uncommon to learn that the person you're talking to has had some similar experience or knows someone in their family who has gone through something similar, which will add to your relief and help you feel less alone.

QUESTIONS

You should expect that the person you're talking to will

have questions. They might ask: How long has this been going on? Did anything change, or did something difficult happen before you started feeling this way? Can you describe what it feels like? You don't have to answer if you don't want to. Just remember that the person is trying to better understand what you're going through. If you feel like they're going in the wrong direction, imagine the question you wish they'd ask, and answer that one!

SOMEONE WHO DOESN'T UNDERSTAND

Even though you've worked hard to choose the best person to talk to, that person might not respond with understanding and kindness. Be ready for that possibility; it happens sometimes. You work up the nerve to share and are told something discouraging or invalidating like "it's just a phase," "you'll get over it," "stop being silly," or "you worry too much." This usually has more to do with the other person's expectations, comfort, and cultural awareness than with their feelings about you. It still feels bad, though. Try to explain how your problems are affecting your ability to live a healthy and happy life. Put it out there that you're having a hard time and aren't sure how to make things better.

If for some reason the person still isn't getting it, remember there's someone else out there who will. You can reach out to a professional resource if you can't find someone in your life who understands. Please don't stop looking for help, and don't ever go back to ignoring your situation or struggling alone.

Talking to Parents and Caregivers

Talking to a parent or caregiver about mental health can be scary for a lot of reasons. Many teens are afraid to tell their caregivers because they don't want to upset them. Caregivers might not understand, may be dismissive, or may become stressed and angry. A good question to ask yourself is how would you feel if someone you love was suffering and came to you? Likely, you would be upset that they were struggling, but you would not be upset with them. You'd be glad they confided in you and would be ready to help them in any way you could. In any event, it's an important conversation that needs to happen. What follows are some of the most common concerns people give for not talking to their parents or caregivers, and some tips for overcoming them.

I DON'T KNOW HOW MY PARENTS OR CAREGIVERS WILL REACT.

If you are concerned about how your caregivers will respond, one option is to schedule a meeting with both of them or with one at a time. Instead of a sudden, potentially unexpected conversation, you can pick a time when they're not busy. This will allow them to think, anticipate, and prepare. Choose a time and place where you are comfortable, and plan what you want to say beforehand. You can plan by writing out a script for what you'd like to say. If a conversation is too scary, write a letter. A letter allows you to say exactly what you want without the pressure of an immediate response. Also, with a letter you won't get interrupted. Check out our sample letter at the end of this chapter. Remember, even if it seems scary, or if your family never talks about these things, you still need to do what's right FOR YOU. Be honest about what you're going through and be specific about the support you need. Focus on actions you would like your parents or caregivers to take or things they can change.

MY PARENTS OR CAREGIVERS WILL BE SAD OR DISAPPOINTED.

It might be hard for your caregivers not to show that they are sad, upset, or disappointed. They might be sad that you are suffering, but this does not mean they are upset with you. In fact, many caregivers are upset because they really do care about you. Caregivers often feel guilty and wonder if there was something they could have done differently that would have prevented you from struggling.

Maybe your caregivers have high expectations, and you're afraid your mental health problems will be a disappointment. It's important to figure out if these expectations are really what's going on in their minds. Maybe they don't actually feel that way. If they do, are these expectations reasonable, or sustainable? These might be new questions for your caregivers. And they don't need to have on-the-spot answers. There will be plenty of time for everyone in the family to reflect, and change.

Another concern you may have is that your caregivers may become angry or dismiss your feelings, both of which are painful experiences, especially when you are already hurting. When dealing with a potential conflict, it's helpful to plan a meeting or to write a letter saying very specifically that you're worried about anger or dismissal. Explain to your caregivers that you're struggling and need extra support. If they still dismiss you, tell them that you're trying to take care of yourself and would like to at least have a discussion with a professional. They may be dismissive toward you out of fear, guilt, or their own feelings about the stigma around mental health problems. You can also show them results from the Mental Health Assessment (in the next chapter).

If your caregivers won't or can't help, you may have to turn to other trusted adults, like a favorite teacher, coach, other family member, or someone else, like the parent of a friend. Even if you don't have anyone, there are still ways to talk about your mental health, and we'll cover that soon. The important thing is: Don't stop looking for help.

MY CAREGIVERS WILL ASK TOO MANY QUESTIONS.

Some caregivers will want to know all the details of what you are experiencing. Share as much or as little as you're comfortable with. You might be unsure of how to describe your feelings. You might be afraid of getting into trouble for certain behaviors. You might want some privacy when first opening up about your struggles. It might help to plan what you are comfortable sharing beforehand. You can tell your caregivers that you would like to take the conversation further with a mental health professional. While it's generally unhealthy to hold things in, it's just as important to make sure you are in a safe space when beginning to open up.

MY CAREGIVERS ALREADY HAVE ENOUGH TO WORRY ABOUT.

All adults have responsibilities and stress, but your health and well-being are important and deserve attention—regardless of what else may be going on with your parents or caregivers. If you're worried about stressing them out too much, pick a time to talk when things are calm. And if there's never a calm time, tell them anyway. Tell them what you're going through, and remember that it's a caregiver's job to take care of you.

ONE OR BOTH OF MY PARENTS OR CAREGIVERS ARE PART OF WHY I AM STRUGGLING.

There are several options for what you can do in this situation. If you trust one caregiver, explain how you are feeling and ask that they either tell or do not tell the other caregiver. Often caregivers may not be willing to withhold something like this from their partner, but you can still ask. And if you feel both are part of the problem—or you only have one caregiver—reach out to another adult you trust, or use the resources in Part Four, Do It Yourself Mental Health. Exceptions to this are if you are currently experiencing physical abuse, sexual abuse, neglect, or suicidal thinking. In any of those cases, tell a trusted adult right away. You can visit www.dorightbykids.org to find out more information on definitions of abuse and neglect, how to make a report, and what happens after you report.

MY PARENTS OR CAREGIVERS WON'T BELIEVE ME.

Even if your caregivers love and respect you, they still might think you're "going through a phase," or dismiss the idea of getting professional help. Of course, ignoring problems because they are unpleasant does not make them go away, and you may need to ask specifically for what you need. You can explain that, even though you hear what they're saying, you want the chance to speak to a mental health professional. If you can't change their minds, you will have to reach out to other adults. These include teachers, relatives, social workers, counselors, and psychologists at school. Any of these people can help you talk to your caregivers or put you in contact with other resources. Even though your caregivers are not validating your struggles, it does not make those struggles unreal or unimportant. If you need professional help, put together a list of reasons why this is the help you need. You can also reach out to friends, online communities, and other accessible mental health resources like apps and online education websites.

WORKSHEET

PREPARING TO SHARE

When you need to have a conversation about hard topics, it's important to plan ahead so you aren't caught off guard and don't lose your ability to express yourself in the way you want. Use this worksheet to ready yourself for sharing.

1. Who do you want to share with? _____

_____

_____

_____

_____

_____

_____

2. What do you want to share? (Use additional pages as needed to write out everything you might share. This will be your script when it's time to have the conversation.) _____

_____

_____

_____

_____

_____

_____

_____

_____

_____

3. What is the best response you could hear after you share?

_____

_____

_____

_____

_____

_____

_____

4. What's the worst response you could hear? What would they say or how would they react that would make you feel worse than you do now? _____

_____

_____

_____

_____

_____

_____

5. What do you need from this person to feel better? Be as clear and specific as you can be. (Example: I need you to listen and not interrupt. I need you to call me once a week to check in. I need you to help me talk to my caregivers.) Add this answer to your script from question 2. _____

_____

_____

_____

_____

_____

_____

6. What are you going to do if the person you're sharing with doesn't respond in the best way? (Examples: talk to another friend, write in your journal, take a walk.) _____

_____

_____

_____

_____

_____

_____

_____

_____

_____

When it's time to have the conversation, use the script you developed from questions 2 and 5. Make sure to ask for what you need, and if you don't get the response you want, leave the conversation and follow your plan from question 6.

WORKSHEET

SAMPLE LETTER TO HELP START A CONVERSATION

Use the letter below and fill in the blanks. Pick from the options we've listed or use your own words.

Dear _____ ,

For the past _____ (day/week/month/year), I have been feeling _____ (unlike myself/sad/angry/anxious/moody/agitated/lonely/hopeless/fearful/overwhelmed/distracted/confused/stressed/empty/restless/unable to function/unable to get out of bed).

I have struggled with _____ (changes in appetite/changes in weight/loss of interest in things I used to enjoy/ hearing things that were not there/seeing things that were not there/feeling unsure if things are real or not real/my brain playing tricks on me/lack of energy/increased energy/inability to concentrate/alcohol or drug use or abuse/self-harm/skipping meals/overeating/overwhelming focus on weight or appearance/feeling worthless/uncontrollable thoughts/guilt/paranoia/nightmares/bullying/not sleeping enough/sleeping too much/risky sexual behavior/overwhelming sadness/losing friends/unhealthy friendships/unexplained anger or rage/isolation/feeling detached from my body/feeling out of control/thoughts of self-harm/cutting/thoughts of suicide/plans of suicide/abuse/sexual assault/death of a loved one).

Telling you this makes me feel _____ (nervous/anxious/hopeful/embarrassed/empowered/proactive/mature/self-conscious/guilty), but I'm telling you because _____ (I'm worried about myself/it is impacting my schoolwork/it is impacting my friendships/I am afraid/I don't want to feel like this/

I don't know what to do/I don't have anyone else to talk to about this/I trust you).

I'd like to _____ (talk to a doctor or therapist/ talk to a guidance counselor/talk to my teachers/talk about this later/create a plan to get better/talk about this more/ find a support group), and I need your help.

Sincerely,

_____ (Your name)

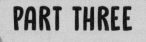

PART THREE

GETTING PROFESSIONAL HELP

THERAPY OFFICE ESSENTIALS

TISSUES

FRAMED DIPLOMA

SO. MANY. BOOKS.

SOME KIND OF PLANT

RIDICULOUSLY COMFORTABLE COUCH

WEIRD ART

FANCY RUG

Let's be honest: It's hard enough to talk to the people closest to you about your mental health. There are so many challenges to overcome: fear, embarrassment, and stigma to name a few. Often, that conversation leads to a decision—to reach out to a mental health professional. The importance of that decision shouldn't be overlooked! It's a big step toward feeling better, and you should give yourself credit for finding the courage to change.

But how do you reach out to a mental health professional? What's the best kind of treatment? And who is the right person to provide it? There are countless other questions, like what if you need medications, or need to go to a hospital? What if you find a therapist but they're not the right one? What if your caretaker doesn't have insurance and can't afford to pay for therapy? Don't worry. We'll cover all of these things and more in this chapter. For now, take comfort that you're in the right place and are about to learn the ins and outs of getting help.

The What, Why, and How of Therapy

WHAT, EXACTLY, IS THERAPY?

Therapy is talking about your problems with a mental health professional. Talking about all of the thoughts, feelings, and behaviors that cause you distress and keep you from feeling well and in control of your life. There are many different types of psychotherapy, but you don't need to worry about that right now. What's important here is to know that talking with a therapist or counselor can help you deal with whatever has been causing you pain or keeping you from enjoying your life.

While in therapy, you'll learn to question your negative thoughts and change your behaviors. Your therapist will encourage you to confront things you've been bottling up. It's challenging emotional work, and some days you might leave the office feeling sad or angry or exhausted. That's all part of the process. Sometimes things get harder before they get easier—but they do get easier.

Not all therapy is problem-focused. Sometimes, just talking to someone who is nonjudgmental can offer an emotional release and a sense of being heard, understood, and supported.

Here are some other reasons to consider therapy:

* To heal pains from the past
* To cope with symptoms
* To understand and deal better with strong emotions like fear, grief, or anger
* To build relationship skills
* To feel stronger in the face of challenges
* To change behaviors that hold you back
* To figure out your goals
* To strengthen your self-confidence
* To build new habits and healthier routines

WHAT IF I'M NOT READY TO SHARE ABOUT SOMETHING THAT HAPPENED OR SOMETHING I'M FEELING?

If your therapist asks you something and you're not comfortable discussing it yet, that's okay. Just explain that you're not ready. Therapists are trained to respect this and give you the time and space you need. As you build trust with your therapist, you'll feel comfortable opening up more and more. Keep in mind that you can't make things better without first talking about them. Your therapist has probably heard it all, so don't worry that you'll seem weird.

HOW DO I FIND A THERAPIST?

Looking for a therapist can be intimidating, but there are plenty of resources to help you. Start by asking around. Check with your friends and family to see if they know anyone to recommend. If they like their therapist, there is a chance you will too. It can be comforting to know someone you trust has already had a good experience with them.

Most likely your caregiver will have to do the legwork of finding a therapist and sorting out insurance and payment.

If they have trouble with this process, they can ask your doctor or religious leader for a referral. Or you could reach out to your school guidance counselor, school social worker, or school psychologist. If you are in college, you can speak with a therapist at your school's counseling center. All of these people are trained mental health professionals and can meet with you at no cost. They may not be able to see you as frequently as a private therapist, but it's a great way to start. (See Resources at the end of the book for more suggestions.)

For now, think about what traits in a therapist might make you feel more comfortable. Some things you might want to consider are:

* **GENDER.** Some people feel more comfortable opening up about their feelings to someone of a particular gender.
* **SEXUAL ORIENTATION.** If you're part of the LGBTQ+ community, you might feel comfortable with a therapist who's part of that community too.
* **RACE, ETHNICITY, AND CULTURE.** In a perfect world, therapists of all backgrounds would be culturally competent—able to understand the unique issues faced by people from cultures other than their own. But sometimes it makes sense to trust someone who shares your ethnic background.
* **LANGUAGE.** If English is your second language, you might benefit

from speaking with someone who is fluent in your first language.

✳ **RELIGION.** Some therapists specialize in providing therapy through a religious or spiritual lens.

✳ **AREAS OF FOCUS/EXPERTISE.** Most therapists are well trained in treating depression and anxiety, but if you're struggling with something specific, such as an eating disorder, addiction, bipolar disorder, or trauma, you can look for someone who specializes in that particular issue.

✳ **AVAILABILITY.** Depending on where you live, it might take weeks to get an appointment. There might be only one therapist in your area who accepts your caretaker's insurance and has openings. Maybe this person doesn't have a lot of experience with the issues you're struggling with or is different from who you'd like in age or background. It's worth giving that person a try anyway. You could be pleasantly surprised.

WHAT WILL MY FIRST SESSION BE LIKE?

Think of your first appointment as a consultation: a chance to meet with the therapist and make sure you're a good fit. Some therapists will even provide a free consultation over the phone before your appointment.

Going to therapy for the first time might make you nervous, and that's normal! But know that your first session is just a conversation. Two people talking. Asking and answering questions. Your therapist will probably start by asking what brings you to therapy, and what you hope to get out of it. They will want to know what you think the problem is, and about your life, your school, and where you live. It is also common to be asked about your family and friends.

WHAT IF I DON'T LIKE MY THERAPIST?

One of the most important factors in therapy is your relationship with the therapist. If something's off in that relationship, it can be hard to make progress. Feeling comfortable with the person you choose is very important; you should be able to develop a sense of trust and safety so that you can speak honestly.

But how do you figure out whether it's a problem with the relationship or instead the fact that therapy can bring up a lot of really uncomfortable feelings? Sometimes, without realizing it, you might transfer your feelings about a person in your life onto your therapist, which can be confusing. Even more confusing is that sometimes things get harder before they get easier. And sometimes we get angry at people who tell us things that are hard to hear even though we need to hear them.

The best way to resolve this confusion is to bring it up with your therapist. Say it out loud in plain language: "I'm not sure if this relationship is working for me." Therapists are trained in overcoming obstacles like this, and they shouldn't take it personally. Sometimes they can recommend another therapist who will be a better fit. Sometimes the conversation itself will uncover an issue you needed to talk about.

If you've given it your best and it's still not working out, there's nothing wrong with looking for a new therapist. But don't give up on therapy completely! Finding the right therapist is a little like dating. You wouldn't go on one bad date and give up on dating entirely, would you? So, why try just one therapist and give up on therapy? Just like with other relationships, it can take time to find the right person.

WHAT CAN I DO TO MAKE SURE MY THERAPY "WORKS"?

To get the most out of your therapy sessions, you'll want to be an active participant. Here's how:

* **KNOW YOUR GOALS FOR TREATMENT. Think about the specific behaviors or issues you care most about and share those with your therapist.**
* **BE HONEST. Your therapist can't really help you if you don't share the whole picture. Don't say you're fine if you're not.**
* **KEEP AN OPEN MIND. Be willing to consider new ways of thinking and behaving. We all resist change, so don't be surprised if you are tempted to quit right before some real changes happen.**
* **IF YOU THINK YOU'RE NOT MAKING PROGRESS, TELL YOUR PROVIDER. A good therapist will be responsive so that you can get the most out of your sessions. After discussing your concerns, if you're still not comfortable, you might meet with another therapist for advice and possibly to switch.**
* **TAKE YOUR THERAPY HOME. Consider keeping a journal to expand on what you've been discussing in therapy. Think about ways to use ideas from therapy in your daily life.**

That must be a joke, right? *Therapy homework?* But to really get the most out of therapy, sometimes your therapist will assign "homework." This will be practical things, like "write down how you feel each day," or "introduce yourself to someone new." Sometimes it will be practicing a specific coping skill you're learning in therapy. If your therapist gives you a homework assignment and you don't feel ready for it, just say so and ask for something more manageable.

HOW LONG DO I NEED TO STAY IN THERAPY?

Most people need more than a few sessions to get the full benefit of therapy. It's common to see a therapist for several months. Some people will stay in therapy for years or leave and come back at different points in their life. Your therapist will work with you to sort this out.

We get it—therapy sounds like a lot of work, and you might not want to go. If you've never gone to therapy before, it might seem too scary or uncomfortable. Or maybe you have seen a therapist, but you had a bad experience. It's okay to not want to go to therapy. Although it can be really helpful, it should never be forced. Fortunately, there are some things you can do other than therapy to improve your mental health. See Part Four for plenty of suggestions.

Online Therapy

Online therapy is similar to regular therapy, except it happens online instead of in an office. Sessions are typically an hour long and can take place weekly or at whatever frequency you and your therapist decide on.

Here are some reasons you might consider online therapy:

* It's hard for you to find time to go into a therapist's office physically.
* You live in a small town where there aren't enough therapists.
* The therapists where you live are all booked and have waiting lists to get in to see them.
* You're more comfortable using an online platform than going into an office to talk to a stranger in person.
* You need more flexible hours than most therapy offices can provide.
* You want the ability to text or email with your therapist between appointments.

Online therapy can be more convenient than traditional therapy, but it's not perfect. Many of the challenges of traditional therapy still apply, such as needing to take the time to find a therapist who's a good fit. It also introduces some new challenges:

* Therapists design their offices to be comfortable, peaceful, private spaces. With online therapy, you'll need to find your own peaceful space.
* If your apartment or house is crowded, it might be possible for others to overhear what you are saying. This can make it potentially harder to share.
* Therapy is all about communication, and there's no perfect substitute for communicating in person. If you're video-chatting, you still get to see some body language and facial expressions. But if you're doing a call without video, you miss out on that. And if you're texting, you also miss out on each other's tone of voice.
* Technology solves a lot of problems, but it also introduces new ones. You'll need a decent Internet connection and a device that can handle the conversation without lag. Even then, there may be technical difficulties from time to time that are outside of your control.

Therapy Apps

There's a growing number of therapeutic apps that might be worth trying, especially if you aren't able to participate in traditional therapy. You may have seen advertisements for services like Talkspace and BetterHelp. At the time of writing this book, these services are not covered by insurance, but that may be changing soon. Each of these apps works differently, but they usually provide some combination of the following:

* MATCHING YOU WITH THE RIGHT THERAPIST. **The app will ask you for some information about yourself and use it to find a therapist who will (hopefully) be a good fit for you. This takes some of the work out of finding a therapist.**
* 24/7 ACCESS TO THERAPY. **Many apps allow you to talk to someone anytime, not just in scheduled weekly sessions. There's a catch, though: You may only be able to do this through text messages, and it might not be with the same therapist every time.**

✳ REGULAR THERAPY SESSIONS. In addition to perks like the ones described above, most of these apps also give you access to more traditional therapy sessions. The frequency and length of the sessions will depend on the app and on your mental health needs.

Text Lines, Hotlines, and Warmlines

Crisis Text Line is free, anonymous, and provides 24/7 support for anyone in crisis. Text MHA to 741741 to connect with a trained volunteer. You can use the service for any situation any time you need support. The goal is to help people in crisis go from a "hot" moment to a "cool-headed calm," and to give them tools to better handle a crisis in the future. How it works is that a crisis counselor will introduce themselves and invite you to text back and forth. You can share at your own pace and decide for yourself what you're comfortable sharing. The counselor will help you sort through your feelings by asking questions and actively listening.

A hotline is a 24/7 service to help if you're having thoughts about hurting or killing yourself or someone else, or if you're in a crisis and need help to calm down and keep safe. To reach the **National Suicide Prevention Lifeline, call 988.** Every call is confidential, and you can be totally anonymous if you'd like. Hotline services are free, and some are offered in multiple languages. (See Resources at the end of the book for suggested hotlines.)

Here's what to expect when you call a hotline: The person you talk to will be either a trained professional or trained volunteer. They may ask questions to get things started, but you get to guide the conversation and talk about whatever you feel comfortable sharing. This means there's no script that's followed; the crisis workers are truly just having a conversation with you and hoping to help you feel better.

At some point in the call, you and the crisis counselor will develop a safety plan and potential interventions. In some cases, that means having a counselor come to your house, brainstorming with you about which family or friends can help you, or scheduling another call to check in with you later. In rare cases, the police may be called, but the crisis worker will do everything they can to de-escalate and help you come up with a safety plan before they involve anyone else. Some people avoid calling because of this fear, but you shouldn't. The goal is to keep you safe and get you connected to resources.

A warmline is another way to have a conversation with someone who can provide support during hard times. You

can call a warmline if you're in crisis or just need someone to talk to. Warmlines are usually not available 24/7 the way hotlines are. They are staffed by trained peers who have been through their own mental health struggles and know what it's like to need help. They are free and confidential, and they're different from crisis lines or hotlines, which are more focused on keeping you safe in the moment and getting you connected to crisis resources as quickly as possible. (That doesn't mean you can't call a warmline when you're in crisis—a warmline may even be able to help you find the best place to go for crisis resources, or help you mentally prepare to seek out more formal treatment.)

Go to warmline.org for a list of warmlines by state.

Medication

Let's talk about medication for a little bit. Some people are afraid to even think about taking medication. They're worried about what it might mean if they need a pill to help with anxiety or depression or other symptoms. Does that mean they're crazy, or broken? Or that they'll need to take meds for the rest of their lives? Not necessarily. Many people find medication to be really helpful in controlling different symptoms. Some people take them for a short time and never need them again, while others take them for years or forever. It's very personal and depends on a lot of different factors that we'll discuss below.

One thing stands clear, though, and can't be stated firmly enough: If you need to take medication—whether for a little while or even for years—it doesn't mean anything about you as a person! You're not broken and there's nothing to explain or feel guilty about.

Medications affect everyone differently. Some may work really well for your friend, but not for you. Or it may work, but the side effects may be too unpleasant. You'll need to consult with your doctor or a psychiatrist to find the best medication for YOU. That means balancing possible benefits with possible side effects. Keep in mind that medications aren't cures. They treat symptoms. If you stop taking them, your symptoms might return.

Medications often work best when they're part of an overall treatment program. Your plan might include psychotherapy, peer programs, and medication. There's always some trial and error involved in finding the right medication. Some medications take a few weeks or as long as two months to work, and sometimes a medication's side effects may start before its benefits. You might have to try more than one medication before you get the right fit, but many people find it's worth the wait.

TYPES OF MEDICATIONS

Antidepressants help reduce feelings of sadness or depressed mood. They may also reduce suicidal thoughts, although some antidepressants have a side effect of increasing suicidal thinking. If you're worried about this—especially if you've been having suicidal thoughts or have experienced that in the past—make sure to bring it up with your doctor. Antidepressants do not make people "happy" or change their personalities. Some antidepressant medications also work to reduce anxiety.

Stimulants are often used to treat ADHD and can help improve concentration and attention span. They can also improve a person's ability to follow directions and can reduce hyperactivity and impulsiveness.

Mood stabilizers are often used to treat bipolar disorder and can help reduce or eliminate extremes of high and low moods and related symptoms. They shouldn't keep you from experiencing the normal ups and downs of life, though. These medications are also used to treat depression that lasts for a long time, that goes away but comes back, or that isn't treated well enough with an antidepressant alone.

Antipsychotic medications are for mental illnesses such as schizophrenia or bipolar disorder that include psychotic symptoms. They're also used for other conditions, such as depression, anxiety, and difficulty sleeping. Antipsychotic medications can help reduce or, in some cases, eliminate hallucinations and very fearful thoughts.

Tranquilizers and sleeping pills can reduce anxiety and insomnia and help you feel more relaxed. Although only some of them are used mostly to help with sleep, they all might cause drowsiness. Usually, these medications are used only briefly because longer use can cause dependency.

DECIDING WHETHER TO TAKE MEDICATION

If you're considering taking medication, talk honestly with your doctor. Discuss your concerns and learn about your options. Not sure how to do that? The following tips can help:

* GET INFORMATION. **Ask your provider how the medication is supposed to help with your specific symptoms and what the possible side effects are. You might even take notes or ask a friend or relative to go with you for emotional support and to help keep track of important information.**
* TALK WITH OTHERS WHO HAVE SIMILAR EXPERIENCES. **Self-help groups can provide great firsthand information. (See Resources at the end of the book.)**
* THINK ABOUT WHAT'S MOST IMPORTANT *FOR YOU!* **Is it relief from a specific symptom while another one is tolerable? Or maybe you're willing to live with one symptom to avoid certain side effects. What are your main goals? How might medication help?**
* **Sometimes the only way to know if a medication is right for you is to** TRY IT. **You may find it helps you feel much better. If not, you can decide to stop taking it.**

GETTING THE MOST OUT OF MEDICATION

Taking medication can get complicated, but there are a few things you can do to make it easier. First, keep track of your progress. Write down your medications and how you're feeling. Write questions too, and share them with your medical providers. This can also serve as a record for the future—if you end up taking different medications, you can look back to see which ones worked and for how long.

If you're experiencing unpleasant side effects, your doctor or pharmacist can help. If your medicine ever makes you feel sick, develop a fever, a skin reaction, or anything else that worries you, don't suffer in silence—call your doctor or pharmacist right away.

Similarly, if you are thinking about stopping your medication, be sure to talk to your doctor and others who support you. They may be able to help you decide. Even if you don't want help with the decision, people close to you should know that you're not feeling well or that you are struggling with side effects.

Stopping medications abruptly can make you feel ill and possibly could cause a seizure. They should be stopped gradually and with help from a doctor.

Lastly, when you take medication, do not use drugs or alcohol. The combination can be dangerous or even deadly.

Hospitalization

Sometimes, hospitalization might be needed for a person to stay safe and be closely monitored, accurately diagnosed, and to have their medications adjusted or stabilized. People are often scared to go to the hospital but find it's not at all what they expected. The goal of hospitalization is not to keep you there indefinitely. The goal is to return you home as soon as you are feeling safe and in control (of both emotions and behavior).

During a hospital stay, you will first have a complete physical examination to determine your overall state of health and for use in building your treatment plan. You always have the right to an explanation of your treatment and to refuse treatment if you feel uncomfortable or unsafe. You also have the right to have your health information protected and kept private through confidentiality.

It's common for people to go to the hospital because of a mental health condition. Sometimes people go specifically because of what the hospital has to offer. Other times, it's just the first place we think of when we are in crisis. Understanding what happens when you check yourself into a hospital can help you decide whether it's the best option for you right now.

If you decide you need to go to a hospital, your treatment options depend on the level of care you will need. Many general hospitals have inpatient psychiatric units that provide 24-hour care. Partial hospitalization provides therapeutic services during the day, but not on a 24-hour basis. It can be an intermediate step between inpatient care and discharge. Residential care is 24-hour psychiatric care, or programs for the treatment of addictions, provided in a residential setting.

HOW CAN A HOSPITAL HELP WITH MENTAL ILLNESS?

There are lots of reasons why people go to the hospital for mental illness. Here are a few:

✳ TO BE SAFE. **Sometimes, if you are having thoughts of hurting or killing yourself, a hospital is needed to provide monitoring by**

people who are trained to keep you and those around you safe. A team will work with you to develop a safety plan, and you will be sent home with follow-up appointments, medications, and new skills and strategies.

* TO ESCAPE FOR A FEW DAYS. Hospital stays for mental health are usually pretty short (from a few days to a week or two). But if your day-to-day life is overwhelming, a short break can go a long way for your mental health. While you're at the hospital, meals are prepared for you, your laundry is done for you, and your meds are given to you by nurses at scheduled times. You may be able to participate in things such as group therapy and art therapy.

* TO GET QUICK, COMPREHENSIVE MEDICAL CARE. Meeting all your mental health needs can feel like juggling way too many things at once. There's medication, therapy, lifestyle changes . . . not to mention your physical health. In a hospital, you can see specialists for all of those things—all in a single day!

* TO SET UP AFTERCARE AND A TREATMENT PLAN. What happens when your hospital stay is done? Well, answering that question is actually *part* of your stay. If you need medications, you'll be given refills and the hospital can make referrals for a therapist and any other specialists you might need to see.

COMMON FEARS ABOUT
A HOSPITAL STAY

Going to the hospital can be frightening, even if you've gone before and know more or less what to expect. There are lots of reasons why, but let's take a look at some common ones:

* **YOU'RE AFRAID OF HITTING ANOTHER LOW POINT.** When people go to the hospital, it's usually because they feel they're at the end of their rope. It might be that low point you're afraid of—not the hospital itself. In that case, you can try to intervene early by taking a look at your self-care, your participation in therapy, and your use of medications.

* **YOU HAD A BAD EXPERIENCE LAST TIME.** Not every hospital is the same. As unfair as it is, it's possible that the hospital you went to last time just wasn't good enough. If you think you might need to go to the hospital again at some point, it might be worth talking to your caregivers about where you want to go and what kinds of treatment you do or don't want to receive. You can also research online to try and find a hospital or program that's a good fit. Many

counties have up-to-date local listings. (See Resources at the end of the book for more suggestions.)

✳ YOU'RE EXPERIENCING INTRUSIVE THOUGHTS. Some people have persistent, unwanted thoughts about bad things happening to them—such as going to the hospital. This can happen even if you're nowhere close to a point where you actually need to be hospitalized. If this sounds like you, talk to someone you trust. If it's a mental health professional, ask the question directly: "Do you think I need to go to the hospital?"

PART FOUR

DIY MENTAL HEALTH

There are many reasons why you might not be able to work with a mental health professional. Therapy can be expensive, and sometimes it's not covered under insurance. In some places, it can be hard to get an appointment. Or maybe you're not ready. But therapy isn't the only way to get help. Fortunately, there are so many things you can do on your own to improve your mental health. Each of the following sections teaches you something different. A few are general and good for just about anyone, like how to deal with loneliness, and managing negative emotions. Others are specific, like how to deal with panic attacks, or what to do if you can't get out of bed.

Getting Out of Bed and Struggling to Leave Your Room

Sometimes the outside world seems too overwhelming, especially when it feels hard enough to be in your own head. It can feel like something is physically preventing you from moving or like there's nothing worth getting out of bed for. Maybe there's too much to do or the world is too loud or you don't feel like you belong. Shame, obligations, or relationships can make you want to sit everything out. When you're feeling and thinking these things, it makes sense that you would want to stay in your room or that you'd feel unable to get out of bed.

Isolation, exhaustion, and lack of motivation or interest in life are common experiences of individuals struggling with stress, depression, anxiety, and other mental health conditions. Almost everyone experiences these to some degree. Hearing this doesn't always help or make things feel easier, however.

Even if your negative thoughts and sensations seem like the only things in the world right now, know that eventually they will pass. You don't have to feel guilty for having the very human experience of struggling. Sometimes the best we can do is to get through one minute at a time under the blankets in our room.

TIPS FOR COPING

* **MAKE A PLAN WITH A FRIEND.** If you feel stuck, text or call someone you care about to make plans. Even if you don't want to share what you're struggling with, a plan can help to get a foot out the door. You could also invite friends or family to come visit you.

* **TEXT OR CALL FOR SUPPORT.** Connecting with other people is important, especially when you're struggling. Reach out to someone you trust to share what's going on with you. Lots of people do not reach out because they feel like a burden, but most people say they would love to support a friend who needs them. If you'd rather not talk about what's happening, that's okay too! Even sharing videos and memes unrelated to what you're experiencing can help you feel less alone.

* **RUN ERRANDS OR COMPLETE SMALL TASKS.** When it's hard to leave your room, small tasks tend to pile up, leading you to want to stay in your room even longer. Think about some of the things you could take care of—like doing laundry, cleaning your room, going food shopping, sending emails, ordering things online, etc. You can set a specific time frame (five minutes, thirty minutes, an hour) to do something that might feel hard but is realistic. Once you start, it's usually a lot easier to keep going.

* **REACH OUT TO A PROFESSIONAL.** If you find you are unable to get out of bed for an extended period of time, think about reaching out to people in your support network or a professional to seek help.

Coping with Panic Attacks

One of the most difficult things about having a panic attack is the intense fear of the experience. It takes over and makes it hard if not impossible to think clearly. On a practical level, this means that the person having the attack will have trouble problem-solving and making decisions. One solution is to learn and practice a few skills that can help when the time comes. Then you won't have to fight the panic, which only makes it worse.

Here are a few things to try:

* TALK TO YOURSELF. Talk out loud. Tell yourself exactly what you need to hear to feel better. "You're going to be okay." "You've been through this before, and you know it's not going to kill you." "You will get through this, and you're stronger than you know." Sing a song.
* BREATHE SLOWLY AND DEEPLY. You'll probably struggle because your body wants to tense up and hyperventi-

late. Gaining control over anxiety and panic is retraining your body and brain to have better responses. It helps to breathe in through your nose and out through your mouth. Purse your lips on the exhale so it makes a noise. See if you can make your stomach rise and fall with each inhalation and exhalation. You can also try counting your breaths like this: three seconds in, five or six seconds out.

* DISTRACT YOURSELF. Count backward by threes from 100. Recite all the words from your favorite song. Count the number of trees outside the window, or the cars parked on the road. Some people have a favorite podcast or playlist that they turn to, but you want to have it cued up and ready.

* USE A GROUNDING TECHNIQUE. Grounding can help you calm your body and mind and stay in the moment. Put your feet flat on the ground and touch your chair or another object. How does it feel? Is it cold? Rough? Does it have patterns? Describe it in your mind or out loud. You can also talk through each of the five senses: "I see—" "I feel—" "I hear—" "I smell—" "I taste—" You don't have to do them in order. You don't even need to make sense. As long as your mind is connecting you to your surroundings and not to anxious thoughts, you're good. Try to find a rhythmic

pattern. Keep talking until you feel your mind and your body calm down.

* REACH OUT. When things are calm again, reach out to others who can support you. It's good to vent, and to find others who share your experiences. This can help you feel less alone and encourage you when what you want to do is run away or criticize yourself.

* SELF-CARE. After an attack, people often feel physically and emotionally exhausted. Have a self-care plan ready, such as resting in a calm quiet place, listening to gentle music, taking a bath, or doing whatever helps you feel safe. Don't feel bad about cancelling any plans.

Battling Loneliness

Humans are social animals—it's in our nature to want to connect with others. When those needs aren't being met, it's completely normal to feel lonely. Loneliness is a universal emotion. We all feel it at one point or another, in our own ways.

Sometimes loneliness comes from feeling disconnected or misunderstood, feeling like you don't "fit in"—with your classmates, with your friends, with society in general. Or maybe you have a group of friends, but wish you had a best friend. Or maybe you have both of those, but miss being in a romantic relationship. Sometimes you might feel lonely after moving to a new city or going through a breakup. And loneliness can also be a sign of depression, anxiety, and other mental health conditions.

Whatever the reason, there are ways to help yourself feel less alone. Here are some tips:

✷ **ACKNOWLEDGE THAT YOU'RE LONELY. Change often starts with admitting how you're feeling—even just to yourself. Try** to identify why and how you're feeling lonely. Once you have a better understanding of your own experience with loneliness, it's a lot easier to figure out what steps to take to feel better.

✳ BOOST THE CONNECTIONS YOU ALREADY HAVE. Loneliness can be all-consuming, making it hard to recognize the relationships that are right in front of you. Do you have classmates who seem nice but who you aren't very close with? Or is there a person you've never really talked to even though you always "like" each other's social media posts? Try reaching out to one of these people, or to a friend you lost touch with a few years ago. You might be surprised at how willing that person is to connect on a deeper level. Even if they don't become your new best friend, hopefully you'll feel a little more con-nected to the people around you.

✳ JOIN A CLUB OR ACTIVITY. It's easier to start a friendship with someone you have something in common with, so try getting involved in activities that revolve around your interests. Find a book club, a sports team, or an art class. You can even start taking a workout class at the same time each week—you'll likely see some of the same faces regularly. And don't forget about online groups! If you can't find a good local group, there's probably a great online community for any hobby or interest you can think of.

* TAKE CARE OF SOMEONE ELSE. What's really missing when you feel lonely is a sense of belonging and purpose. Helping others can make you feel needed. Maybe you have a neighbor or family member who would love someone to vent to. Or see if your local retirement home or animal shelter (yes, puppies and kittens count as "someone else") could use a helping hand. Giving back to your community is a great way to feel less alone in the world.

* SPEND TIME IN PUBLIC. If having a conversation sounds intimidating, do your best to just get out in public. Being around others, even if you don't interact with them, can lessen the intensity of your loneliness. If you need to get homework done, head to the library instead of doing it in your bedroom. Planning to mindlessly scroll on your phone for thirty minutes? Go grab a snack and a table at your favorite coffee shop and spend your social media break there.

* ENJOY YOUR OWN COMPANY. Being alone doesn't have to mean being lonely. Community is important, but so is your relationship with yourself. Make sure you're speaking to yourself kindly and giving yourself the same credit that you'd give someone else. Lean into the solo activities you enjoy: Work your way through that list of movies you've been meaning to

watch or get yourself a starter kit for that new hobby you want to pick up. Take time to reconnect with who you truly are: your strengths, your goals, and anything that makes you, *you*. Bonus: When you get to know yourself better, it's easier to feel good about yourself when you do go out and socialize.

Dealing with Self-Hate

Maybe you don't like the way you look. Or maybe you feel like you've let people down, or you don't have any friends. You might feel like you're stuck in a downward spiral: The more you hate yourself, the more you mess up, and then you hate yourself even more. So how do you get unstuck?

It helps if you can identify where the feelings of self-hatred are coming from. There are lots of things that affect the way we feel about ourselves. Here are a few:

* EXTREME SELF-CRITICISM. A little bit of constructive self-criticism can help you notice your mistakes and correct them. But once it starts making you feel bad about yourself, it's no longer useful.
* UNREALISTIC EXPECTATIONS. If you're constantly falling short of your own expectations, it might be time to reevaluate them. "Lowering your expectations" might sound like a bad thing, but you're not doing yourself any favors by keeping your expectations impossibly high.

* **COMPARISON WITH OTHERS.** It's easy to compare your weaknesses with everyone else's strengths. Sure, you have flaws and have made mistakes . . . but so has everyone else, including those you look up to and admire the most. Social media makes it easy for these people to hide their flaws and show only their successes. Comparing yourself to them is doubly unfair.

* **MISTAKES FROM THE PAST.** Maybe you're holding a grudge against yourself for something you did a long time ago. There's nothing you can do to change the past, but you can always learn from it and move forward.

* **FEELING OUT OF PLACE.** It's important to find a group of people who are supportive and appreciate you. This could take some time, but it's worth the effort and those people *do* exist. Some people don't find their crowd until college or after starting a job. And for others it happens online.

* **FORCE OF HABIT.** Once you make a habit of criticizing yourself, it can be hard to stop. "I hate myself" or other negative self-talk can sometimes be an intrusive thought—something that just pops into your mind with no real meaning behind it.

WHAT NOW?

Accept yourself and where you are right now. It's okay to hate yourself; it's not unusual to do so. You might be surprised at the people around you who secretly hate themselves—often it's people you look up to and love. And just like those people, you too are worthy of love.

As you learn to feel better about yourself, you will become happier. It's a process that takes time. Here are a few tips for improving your self-image:

* **START SMALL. You don't have to absolutely love yourself right away. Start by having compassion for yourself. Practice being kind to yourself. You don't have to like someone to be nice to them. You also don't have to like every single thing about yourself. Start by finding one or two small things that you do like about yourself, and spend more time thinking about those.**
* **DON'T DEFINE YOURSELF BY YOUR FLAWS OR MISTAKES. Flaws are things everyone has. Mistakes are things everyone makes. Neither are who you are.**
* **PRACTICE POSITIVE SELF-TALK. Say positive things about yourself—out loud, just to yourself. They don't have to be big**

things right away. Maybe you're not ready to say "I am smart" or "I am beautiful." But if you're reading this, you can truthfully say "I am working on myself." It's not about where you are; it's about which direction you're going in.

✳ ACCEPT OTHER PEOPLE'S COMPLIMENTS. When people say nice things about you, don't argue or roll your eyes. Just say "thank you." Try to believe that they mean it. Consider why they might have a point. You can add this to your positive self-talk: "So-and-so told me I'm good at . . ."

✳ IMPROVE YOUR MENTAL HEALTH. Feelings of self-hatred are classic symptoms of depression. If you treat the underlying depression, your self-image will improve too.

Dealing with Suicidal Thinking

If you are struggling with suicidal thoughts, there are a few things you should know. First, you are not alone. Many people have thoughts about dying at different times in their lives. Just know that it does get better. Even if you're feeling lost and hopeless, those feelings will change, and there are things you can do to move toward recovery.

WHAT DO I DO IF I DON'T WANT TO DIE BUT I DON'T WANT TO LIVE?

Not everyone who thinks about dying wants to die. Many people think about dying to help manage or end mental and emotional pain. There's a difference between passive and active suicidal thoughts. Passive suicidal thoughts are thoughts you have about dying without actually having a plan. Active suicidal thinking includes making plans to end your life.

It's important to understand when passive suicidal thoughts become harmful to your safety. Consider the feelings behind these thoughts. Understanding the source can help you better manage the thoughts and prevent a crisis from occurring. Here are a few examples:

SUICIDAL THINKING FEELS LIKE ...

" I'VE BEEN TRAPPED BY A GIANT BOA CONSTRICTOR."

* **YOU'RE FEELING DEPRESSED.** A common symptom of depression is thinking about death. It might be a fixation on the terrible things in the world, how things will end, or what the purpose of life is. When you're depressed, negative thoughts are "stickier." Treating the underlying depression can help you focus on more positive thoughts.

* **YOU'RE EXPERIENCING OBSESSIVE OR INTRUSIVE THOUGHTS.** Obsessive thoughts of death can come from anxiety as well as depression. They might include worrying that you or someone you love will die. Intrusive thoughts can start out as harmless passing thoughts that you then become fixated on because they scare you. If this sounds like you, it might help to read about dealing with thinking traps on page 159.

* **YOU'RE GRIEVING.** Our natural curiosity about death becomes more personal when we are experiencing grief. Maybe you lost a family member, a friend, or a pet. When someone you care about dies, it's natural to think about what that means. You might be wondering about what death really is, what's happened to your loved one . . . and what will happen to *you* when you die. Give yourself plenty of time to grieve. Many people find comfort in watching TV shows or movies about grief and loss, reading books or poetry about it, or talking to a spiritual leader or anyone else

you trust about what you're going through. Writing down your feelings in a journal might also be a help.

OTHER REASONS FOR THINKING ABOUT DYING

✳ **HOPELESS?** At your lowest, your mind can search out and find all the bad things in your life. Or maybe it's just one problem but there's no easy or doable solution. Or the obvious solution is blocked by another problem. And so on. The pain of this kind of situation can be very intense, but try to remember that hopelessness is both a feeling and a judgment. Feelings don't last forever, and judgments can't be trusted when you're in distress. All the more reason to ask the opinion of someone you trust.

✳ **EXHAUSTED?** Maybe life has thrown so much at you that you feel like you don't have the energy to go on. It is okay to want to take a temporary break from reality. The key word here is *temporary*. Taking time to focus on self-care is actually a selfless act: When you take care of yourself, you have more energy to give to others. But it's also okay and important to take care of yourself just for you, not for others.

* **SOCIALLY ISOLATED?** Isolation often leads to feelings of loneliness and can increase the likelihood of suicidal thoughts. Try reaching out to family for weekly calls, start a virtual club with some friends, or gain comfort by spending time with pets. It's important to remain socially connected in some way.

* **RECKLESS?** Maybe the things that keep you safe, like seat belts, no longer mean much to you. Are you intentionally or unintentionally putting yourself in harm's way? If so, recognize that you're not making safe decisions. Reach out and find someone you trust. Tell them, and ask them for help.

* **AFRAID OF BEING A BURDEN?** It's common for people struggling with their mental health to think they are a burden to others—that their mood or behavior is extra work for the people in their life. It's not. If you're reading this and having a hard time believing it, ask: If your friend was struggling with suicidal thinking, wouldn't you want to help? The thing to do now is change the thought from "I'm a burden" to "I need help." Try to surround yourself with friends, family, or other people who support you.

* **FEELING UNSAFE DUE TO PAST TRAUMA?** Sudden life changes and trauma may lead to fear and suicidal thoughts. Name the feelings you're experiencing, and don't judge yourself. Those feelings don't mean anything about you as a person other

than that you're in crisis. Find someone you trust who can help you create a safety plan. Use the worksheet on page 149.

☀ MEDICATION SIDE EFFECTS? Taking certain medications can produce suicidal thoughts as a side effect. If you think this might be happening, call your doctor or pharmacist right away.

If you have been thinking about death and have a plan or intend to make a plan, you do have to tell someone! Having a conversation about suicide can be difficult and intense—and it is a courageous step. If you're nervous about doing this, that's okay, but tell yourself now that it's a must. **YOU DO HAVE TO TELL SOMEONE!** How? It starts with a hard conversation with the right person. **YOU ARE TOO IMPORTANT NOT TO.** Your life is bigger than this moment. Keep reading and we'll walk you through the decisions of who to tell and what to say.

FIRST, WHO TO TELL

☀ RIGHT NOW, TELL SOMEONE WHO IS CLOSE BY. If you're at home, tell a parent, caregiver, sibling, friend, or neighbor. If you're at school, tell a teacher, counselor, the school

nurse, or even a friend. If there are several people available, choose the one you feel most comfortable with.

✳ IF YOU'RE ALONE, DON'T WAIT. Seek out one of the above
people. Call or text them. You can also call your therapist,
if you have one, or your doctor. If no one picks up your
call, you can leave a message, and then keep on calling. Keep
reaching out until you talk to someone. It'll be okay if you
end up with two or three people who are aware of what
you're going through and willing to help.

✳ CALL THE NATIONAL SUICIDE PREVENTION LIFELINE AT 988 if you
don't have a person to contact. Every call is free and confidential and you can be totally anonymous if you'd like.
You can share as much or as little as you choose to about
your experience, and it's a safe space to share. It's offered
in multiple languages too. If you can't call, then text MHA
to 741-741 to reach someone from Crisis Text Line.

WHAT DO I SAY?

Telling someone that you are suicidal is an incredibly difficult and brave act. It takes a lot of courage to share your
thoughts with another person. Start by filling in the blanks

below, and that will give you a script. Use the script to make the conversation easier.

* **For the past** _____ (day/week/month/year), I have been thinking about suicide.
* **I think about dying** every_____ (minute/hour/day/week.)
* **I have been feeling** _____ (hopeless/trapped/unbearable pain/moody/empty/like a burden/angry/anxious/agitated/reckless/isolated).
* **I have struggled with** _____ (eating/sleeping/self-harm/driving recklessly/drinking more/having severe mood swings/overwhelming sadness/unexplained anger or rage).
* **I have thought about** _____ (a plan/a method/how I am going to kill myself).
* **I would like to** _____ (talk to a doctor or therapist/create a safety plan/find a support group) and I need your help.

GIVE YOURSELF SOME CREDIT

If you're reading this section, there's a part of you that wants to feel safer and work toward having a better, more meaningful life. Appreciate yourself for that! It's an important beginning. Try to nurture that part of you, to make it stronger. Think about a reason you *don't* want to die. It doesn't have to be some deep sense of purpose—it could be as simple as not wanting to miss the next season of your favorite show. Acknowledge one small reason to keep going, and build on that. Build up your supports too, which could include people—professionals, friends, and family—activities, self-care routines, and anything that helps add meaning to your life. Mostly, though, remember that your feelings will change and things will get better.

WORKSHEET

FEELING SAFE

Experiencing a traumatic event of any kind can leave you feeling unsafe or unstable. Finding ways to focus on safety and building a sense of control over aspects of life can help you feel more grounded. When we lack safety, we may feel anxious, overwhelmed, or depressed. Use this worksheet to think through how you can increase feelings of security in your life.

BUILDING AWARENESS

Are there situations in life that make you feel out of control?
(Example: having an unexpected conversation or visit, getting into an argument, having to do something you don't
want to do) _____

_____

_____

_____

_____

_____

What are some of the thoughts that go through your mind that
increase negative feelings or experiences? (Example: I don't
know what to do, everything is going to go wrong) _____

_____

_____

_____

_____

_____

_____

What are some of the physical symptoms in your body that increase negative experiences? (Example: my heart races, I get a stomachache, I sweat) _____

_____

_____

_____

_____

BUILDING SAFE COPING SKILLS

What are some positive words you can say to yourself to feel better? _____

_____

_____

What are some things that have helped you feel safe in the past? This can be an action you've taken to reduce negative physical reactions, or an object that feels safe. (Example: holding a stuffed animal, reading your favorite book, listening to calming music) _____

_____

_____

Think of a place where you have felt safe in the past. Take a moment to close your eyes, take a few slow deep breaths, and visualize the place. Think through the details. What do you see, hear, smell, feel, or even taste? _____

_____

_____

_____

_____

Who in your life can you talk to when you feel unsafe or unstable? _____

_____

_____

_____

_____

RADICAL ACCEPTANCE

ACKNOWLEDGE YOUR FEELINGS

LISTEN TO YOUR FEELINGS

FEEL YOUR FEELINGS

ACCEPT YOUR FEELINGS

WORKSHEET

PRACTICING RADICAL ACCEPTANCE

Many times, bad things happen and you have no control over the situation. You can't change people's behaviors or the reality of what is happening, and these experiences are painful. Radical acceptance is a practice that helps you look at situations differently and get some distance from unpleasant emotions like resentment, anger, hatred, or shame. It helps you dial down your emotional pain so you can stay cool, think better, and keep your dignity.

Sounds pretty good, doesn't it? Well, it is and it's actually not that mysterious or complicated, although it does take some practice. The benefits far outweigh the cost of learning, especially when you think of it as a skill you can use for the rest of your life. Use this worksheet to learn how to practice Radical Acceptance.

What's bothering you? The first part of Radical Acceptance is to say clearly what's going on. Why you're upset. Think of an event or situation. It could be recent, or from a while ago. Whatever it is, write down your thoughts about it. _____

_____

_____

_____

_____

_____

Understanding reality. The second part of Radical Acceptance is to separate *reality* from *opinion*. These questions will help you understand the reality of what you are experiencing:

Look at what you wrote above. Is there something there that's a part of reality you have to accept (rather than a judgment or opinion)? For instance, "It shouldn't be this way" is an opinion; "It is this way" is a reality. Write it here: _____

_____

_____

_____

_____

_____

Think about the reality you just described, and sit with it. If a strong feeling comes up, that's okay. Sit with that too.

What events led to this reality? ("This is how things happened.")

_____

_____

_____

_____

_____

Accepting reality. The last part of Radical Acceptance is to accept the reality you've been fighting against. These questions will help:

Think about this reality. Can you accept this reality in your thoughts? What can you tell yourself to help you accept it?

_____

_____

_____

_____

_____

Imagine what it would feel like to accept it. How might you feel if you could let go of the resistance to this reality? Do you think it would feel good? Weird? Might you feel "lighter"? (It's okay too if you can't imagine it at all. This is a new skill that will take practice to learn.) _____

_____

_____

_____

_____

_____

Think again about this reality. Can you accept it in your body? Where are you carrying the resistance to accept this reality? In your shoulders or your back? Is there tension or physical pain? Practice feeling your emotions in your body and then practice releasing them. Write down what that feels like.

_____

_____

_____

_____

_____

_____

_____

Do you feel disappointment, sadness, or grief right now? Sit with that. Acknowledge it. Allow yourself to feel these feelings. Understand that it's okay. You don't have to do anything to change your feelings or make them go away. Just sit with them for a moment. If the feelings pass, notice that too. Write it down here. _____

_____

_____

_____

_____

_____

Despite the painful emotions connected to this reality, if you sit with them and accept them, eventually other thoughts and feelings will emerge. And with them will come other possibilities. Think about other aspects of your life apart from the reality you are working so hard to accept. What about these other aspects of your life are good or meaningful or interesting? Write about this. _____

_____

_____

_____

_____

If you find yourself struggling at this point, write down some pros and cons of accepting this reality. Then go back to the beginning the next time you experience a difficult situation.

_____

_____

_____

_____

_____

_____

Keep in mind that this is a skill to practice and work on throughout your life. It's not something you master the first time! But the payoffs are huge, so do stick with it.

Avoiding Thinking Traps

When life is hard, you start to see the world through a negative lens. It can feel like everything is terrible and there's no way out. You might not be able to change the people around you, or the situation, but you can learn to think more clearly and positively. And that makes it much easier to enjoy life and find solutions to your problems.

HOW DO OUR THOUGHTS GET STUCK IN THE FIRST PLACE?

The world is a complicated place and growing more complicated. Every day we encounter new situations that our cave-dwelling ancestors never had to deal with—school, dating, learning to drive, college applications . . . It's all a lot to process, and our little animal brains are doing the best they can!

Here's a weird fact: Our brains actually don't want to do a lot of thinking and problem-solving. It takes too much energy. Instead, our brains prefer to use mental shortcuts. These shortcuts keep us from getting overwhelmed by too many details and decisions. They help us use past experiences to predict the future. Most of the time this is a good thing. But sometimes, the shortcuts hold us back, especially when they lead us to distort reality and believe things that aren't true.

An example of this is when you try something new and fail. Instead of seeing this as part of the learning process, you say, "I suck. I'm no good at anything. I shouldn't even try!" Your brain is actually trying to protect you from future disappointment. The problem is that the statement—I'm no good at anything; I shouldn't even try—is just not true. The long-term consequences are that you end up feeling bad about yourself, and it becomes almost impossible to learn new things.

BREAKING FREE OF THINKING TRAPS

Each of us is unique, and so are our thoughts. Even so, we tend to get stuck in very similar patterns of thinking. These patterns are called thinking traps. They're also known as thinking errors or automatic negative thoughts (ANTs). Everyone gets caught in these traps sometimes—but with help, you can learn to break free of them!

Breaking free of thinking traps is all about reframing your thoughts. When you reframe a thought, you look for new ways to think about what's bothering you. Sometimes this is all it takes to make a difference in how you feel. It takes practice to learn how to reframe your thoughts. But with time, you can learn to not only think more positively, but to actually change the things you believe about yourself.

While you're learning to reframe your thoughts, don't beat yourself up. Everyone gets stuck in thinking traps. Getting out of them takes time, and you'll probably mess up along the way. Keep in mind that you don't have to hide your feelings to reframe your thoughts. If you feel sad about a breakup, you can tell yourself a more positive version of the story—while still being sad that it happened.

COMMON THINKING TRAPS, AND STRATEGIES FOR GETTING UNSTUCK

* ALL-OR-NOTHING THINKING. This means you see things as good or bad, with nothing in the middle. There is no gray area—just the extremes. "Either I'm the best, or I'm the worst." "I'm either going to get into the perfect college, or be a total loser." "If I don't get an A+, I might as well have gotten an F."

* OVERGENERALIZATION. This means taking a single event and making sweeping conclusions. Example: "I had an argument with my best friend. I'm sure she doesn't want to be friends ever again."

* DISCOUNTING THE POSITIVE. You ignore when good things happen by insisting they "don't count" because there were other circumstances. This allows your brain to stay in a pattern of negative thinking. Example: "I got an A on the exam but so did a lot of other people, and it was graded on a curve."

* JUMPING TO CONCLUSIONS. Jumping to conclusions is when you skip steps in your logic. You take things personally when they really have nothing to do with you. You assume that something bad will happen or that someone will have negative feelings toward you, even though there's no evidence to support that thought. Example: "They didn't text right back. They're mad at me about something and don't like me anymore."

DISCOUNTING THE POSITIVE

★ **"SHOULD" STATEMENTS.** You focus on how things should have gone or should have been rather than how they actually are. Example: "I should exercise more." When you direct "should"

statements toward others, you can feel anger, frustration, and resentment. Example: "He shouldn't have said that to me. He's so inconsiderate."

* BLAMING. You lay blame for things that go wrong entirely on other people, without thinking about where *you* may have gone wrong or how you could have changed a situation. Example: "I got a crappy grade on the test because he was supposed to call me to study together. He knew I needed help to pass the test, so that grade's on him. It's his fault."

* FILTERING. This is when you ignore anything that contradicts what you already believe. If you think "no one ever appreciates me," you ignore compliments. If you think "I'm a failure," you blame yourself for everything bad—and attribute everything good to randomness or luck.

TIPS FOR DEALING WITH THINKING TRAPS

* REFRAME. Think of a different way to view the situation. If your negative thought is "I can't do anything right," a kinder way to reframe it is "I messed up, but nobody's perfect." Or even better, "I messed up, but now I know to pre-

pare for next time." It can be hard to do this when you're feeling down on yourself, so ask yourself what you'd tell a friend if they were saying those things.

* PROVE YOURSELF WRONG. Look for evidence that contradicts a particular negative thought. Think of a time when things *did* turn out well for you. Moving forward, spend more time looking for this different, positive version of what you used to believe. Every time you do this, you're changing the story about yourself. And this is worth doing, because you totally deserve to have a better story!

* REWRITE THE SCENE. This works really well to combat blaming. Imagine the situation is a story or a scene in a movie, and rewrite it so that you're the only character. Only *you* can change the outcome. For example, if you've been thinking that your bad grade on a test was because a friend was supposed to call you to study and didn't, rewrite the story so that you acted differently and there was a positive outcome.

* REMEMBER THAT THOUGHTS AREN'T FACTS. Your thoughts and feelings are valid, but they don't always reflect reality. For example, you might feel ugly, but that doesn't mean you are. Identify where your thoughts and feelings and expectations are coming from. Then ask yourself these questions: Who says you should act a certain way? Are they a true expert on that

subject, and are they entitled to control you? Are their expectations realistic? Does it actually matter what they think? What do *you* want?

* GET SOMEONE ELSE'S PERSPECTIVE. Sometimes other people are able to see our thinking traps better. Therapists are trained to spot thinking traps and help us get unstuck, but friends and family can do it too. Talk to a person you trust, and make sure it's someone who will give you constructive feedback in a positive, caring way. You want them to help you reframe your thoughts without invalidating your feelings.

* WRITE IT OUT. Whether it's in a journal, an online help forum, or on a scrap of paper, writing things down can help shift your perspective a little. After writing, look at your notes as if they're someone else's thoughts. What would you tell a friend who was saying such negative things about themselves? How would you help them focus on the positives?

* COMPLETE THE WORKSHEET ON THE NEXT PAGES: DEALING WITH WORST-CASE SCENARIOS. The key is to keep practicing reframing your thoughts until it becomes a habit!

WORKSHEET

DEALING WITH WORST-CASE SCENARIOS

One of the most common thinking traps is catastrophic thinking, when you immediately jump to the worst-case scenario, usually without all the facts. Examples are: "If I fail this test, I won't get into a good college, and my life will be over" and "I'm a loser. No one is ever going to love me." When you think this way (and we all do at one time or another), you can easily get pulled into a rut. And if it becomes a pattern, you might experience worsened mood, avoidance of responsibilities, and increased anxiety.

Use this worksheet to help reframe catastrophic thinking traps.

List your own examples of worst-case-scenario thinking. Don't worry if it's "truly" a catastrophic thought. Just write down the first things that come to mind. Try to list at least six examples. _____

_____

_____

_____

_____

_____

_____

_____

_____

_____

_____

_____

_____

_____

_____

_____

_____

_____

Look at what you wrote above. Pick three that you want to address. Write them below.

1. _____

_____

_____

2. _____

_____

_____

3. _____

_____

_____

Question each thought by exploring the following:

☀ Are you sure the thought is true or will happen?
☀ Is there any evidence it is true?
☀ Is there evidence it is not true?
☀ Is the thought more rooted in your feelings or reality?
☀ If it is reality, are you able to cope with it? Have you coped with it before?

Look back at your three thoughts. How can you change them to be more realistic and positive? For example, you could change "If I fail this test, I won't get into college" to "One bad test score won't actually change anything, and besides, most of the time when I think I failed, I really didn't."

1. _____

_____

_____

2. _____

_____

_____

3. _____

_____

_____

Now write your reframed thoughts on paper or Post-its and put them where you are most likely to struggle with worst-case-scenario thinking, such as by your bed, in the bathroom, or even on the back of your phone.

Managing
Difficult Emotions

EMOTIONAL
BAGGAGE

Learning to deal with difficult emotions is hard. When people are in emotional pain, they're often willing to do almost anything to make that pain go away. The problem is, what works in the short term is often very harmful or destructive in the long term. Let's start by learning about some of the harmful ways that people deal with difficult emotions.

DENIAL

Denial is when a person refuses to accept that anything is wrong or that help may be needed. When people deny that they are having problematic feelings, those feelings can bottle up until that person ends up "exploding" or acting out in a harmful way.

WITHDRAWAL

Withdrawal is when a person doesn't want to be around other people or participate in activities they used to enjoy. This is different from wanting to be alone from time to time, and can be a warning sign of depression. Some people may withdraw because being around others takes too much energy, or they feel overwhelmed. Others may withdraw because they don't think people like them or want them to be around. In some cases, people who are ashamed of something they've been doing may withdraw so other people don't find out about it. But withdrawal brings its own problems: extreme loneliness, misunderstanding, anger, and distorted thinking. We need to interact with other people to keep ourselves balanced.

BULLYING

Bullying is when a person uses force, threats, or ridicule to show power over others. People typically take part in bullying behavior because they don't feel good about themselves and making someone *else* feel bad makes *them* feel better. It is harmful to both the bully and the person being bullied and does not address underlying issues.

SELF-HARM

Self-harm can take many forms, including: cutting, starving oneself, bingeing and purging, or participating in other dangerous behavior. Many people self-harm because they feel like it gives them control over emotional pain. Although these behaviors may bring temporary relief, they can become addictive and cause greater pain in the long run.

SUBSTANCE USE

Substance use is the use of alcohol and other drugs to make a person feel better about or numb to painful situations. Alcohol and drug use can damage the brain, causing it to need higher amounts of substances to get the same effect. This can make difficult feelings even worse and, in some cases, can lead to suicidal thoughts or addiction. If you are concerned about your use of drugs or alcohol, talk to someone you trust to get help.

If you've been turning to any of those approaches, try following these steps to deal with your difficult emotions more safely:

✳ ACKNOWLEDGE WHEN YOU'RE NOT FEELING GREAT. **Emotional awareness is when you recognize and acknowledge your feelings. Having good emotional awareness lets you under-**

stand what's going on inside of you so you don't get pushed into a reaction that doesn't serve you well. The trick is to name what you're feeling accurately, without judgment or self-criticism. Here's an example: "I'm actually really disappointed that I didn't get invited to the party. I feel sad about it." Spend a day or two observing your thoughts and actions. How do they clue you in to your emotional state? Write these observations in a journal as a first step toward greater emotional awareness.

* ALLOW YOURSELF TO FEEL ALL OF YOUR EMOTIONS. People often do things to try to feel better when they're sad, angry, anxious, embarrassed, or otherwise in pain. This might be a natural reaction, but it's important to let yourself feel your emotions as they arise rather than immediately trying to change them. In other words, take some time to sit with your feelings. It can be uncomfortable, but it's an important step for working through them. This doesn't mean that you should let yourself be angry or devastated for days on end. If you are feeling this way and aren't able to let go of your emotions or work through them, seek help from a trusted friend, family member, or therapist.

* EXPRESS YOUR EMOTIONS IN A DIFFERENT, HEALTHIER WAY. After you have learned to spot the mental and physical cues of

your emotions, you can then find positive ways of express-ing them, such as talking to others, or writing in a journal. Over time, you can look back on these entries to see if any patterns emerge. Extra points if you use your journal not just for venting, but for problem-solving too. Other ways to express your feelings? Cry if you need to. Or watch a movie, read a book, or listen to music that evokes what you're feeling and helps you shed those tears.

✴ **RELEASE THE TENSION.** Anger can be one of the most difficult emotions to express because what you do when you are angry may hurt your relationships. Instead, consider a vigorous workout, going for a run, or even screaming into a pillow. If you're in the middle of a conversation, take a break and come back when you can express yourself appropriately. Avoid accusations and use "I feel" statements to take ownership of your anger or other feelings. For instance, say "I feel hurt and angry when you speak to me that way" instead of "You make me so angry. You're such a jerk!"

✴ **ALLOW YOURSELF TO HAVE POSITIVE *AND* NEGATIVE EMOTIONS.** Both positive and negative emotions are essential. Everyone likes to express joy, excitement, and love. But you may have been taught to push away negative emotions like anger, shame, and frustration. Bottling up your emotions won't make them go away—in fact, they will most likely only get worse. Suppressed emotions can contribute to mental health conditions like anxiety or depression. In some situations, negative emotions are necessary: They give you information about what's important to you and what you might need to change about yourself or your environment.

✳ NEED MORE STRATEGIES? See Resources at the end of the book for more suggestions.

Escaping Toxic Influences

TOXIC INFLUENCES

We all have lots of positive and negative influences in our lives, and sometimes the balance can tip in the wrong direction. In the case of friendship, you might have a friend who is always available and likes to do the same things as you, but they're really sarcastic and negative. Or maybe they say mean or hurtful things. And more and more, when you spend time with this person you come away feeling angry and resentful. You ask yourself, "Why would a friend say such things and act that way?"

Many times, the effects of a toxic relationship will hit you later, *after* a conversation or exchange. You might replay it in your head, wondering why the person acted that way. You might even doubt yourself, or criticize yourself for not handling it differently. Even worse, you might think you're overreacting or being crazy. The extreme form of this is gaslighting, which is a type of emotional manipulation. In gaslighting, a person tries to control you by making you think your reaction or memory is wrong.

As bad as it feels to be in a toxic relationship or situation, there are many things you can do to make it better and pull away. The first step is to let yourself off the hook. Toxic people are really good at what they do! They often mix a few positives in with the negatives, which can be confusing. It's helpful to learn more about toxic people so you can identify them and keep a safe distance. Here are some common traits:

* **MANIPULATIVE.** Toxic people may seem to be genuinely interested in your company and getting to know you. Eventually, they will use the knowledge they gain about you to try and control you. They will often twist your words or make you feel guilty in order to get their way.
* **CRUEL.** Insults are the most direct way that toxic people can make you feel bad, but most of the time they cut into your self-esteem in more subtle ways. When you are feeling happy or proud of yourself, they will find ways to downplay your achievements. They might also act as if they are smarter or superior in an attempt to make you feel insignificant.
* **JUDGMENTAL.** Everyone can be judgmental from time to time, but a toxic person is judgmental almost all the time. They tend to have very strong views and criticize anything that they don't agree with or approve of, instead of considering the circumstances or the feelings of other people.
* **PASSIVE-AGGRESSIVE.** This behavior is expressing discontent without saying it directly. It's a type of hostility that is less obvious than anger and can be shown in a number of different ways. Some forms of passive aggression include

snide comments, sabotaging your efforts, and purposefully doing something—or not doing something—to inconvenience you or get you upset.

* SELF-CENTERED. Toxic people care mostly about themselves. They believe they are better than everyone else and don't think about how their actions affect others. Someone who is self-centered is focused on getting what they want and is unlikely to compromise or consider another person's point of view.

* EXPLOSIVE. In this case, the littlest thing can trigger a fit of rage, and the toxic person may say nasty, hurtful things. If they apologize the next day, they are often insincere and will soon repeat the behavior.

* CONTROLLING. One of the most dangerous traits of a toxic person is controlling behavior. They may try to limit your interaction with friends or family, or keep you from spending time apart from them.

ABUSIVE RELATIONSHIPS

If you are in a situation where someone is trying to restrict your movements or communication, this is abuse and requires immediate action. Call 1-800-799-7233 (or 1-800-787-3224 for TTY), or if you're unable to speak on the phone, you can log onto thehotline.org or text "LOVEIS" to 22522.

One of the problems with abusive relationships is it can be hard to tell what's really going on, especially if the person is subtly controlling and your self-esteem is low. But abusive relationships tend to follow the same stages and signs. They begin by feeling incredibly exciting, with your new friend or romantic partner going out of their way to show their attention and devotion. The relationship often moves very quickly. You're constantly texting and talking to each other. And at first, it's sweet how protective they are of you—how they get a little jealous if you spend time with anyone else, even friends. But then the protectiveness turns into possessiveness and paranoia. In an effort to prove your devotion to them, you start spending less time with other people and giving up your own interests and activities. As a result, you become more and more dependent on this friend or partner, who is using unpredictable affection, criticism, guilt trips, and other forms of manipulation as tools to control you. You feel like you're walking on eggshells around them to avoid offending, upsetting, or enraging them.

WORKSHEET

DETOXIFY YOUR LIFE

Now that you know more about toxic relationships and the traits of toxic people, how do you break free from them? Setting boundaries is a big part of it, but this is harder than it sounds. Setting boundaries is when you take responsibility for your emotions and behaviors but not for other people's.

The questions below will help you set up good boundaries. There are two steps. First, you will make sense of the positive and negative aspects of the influences in your life. Second, you will build confidence to make positive changes that might be uncomfortable or difficult.

IDENTIFY TOXIC INFLUENCES

What or who is the thing that you need to eliminate from your life? This can be a person, behavior, or situation. _____

_____

_____

_____

What is toxic or unacceptable about that person, behavior, or situation? (Examples: "Hitting each other." "Name calling." "Making plans, cancelling, and then going out with someone else.") _____

_____

_____

_____

What are some desirable or healthy alternatives? (Examples: "I want someone who encourages me." "I want someone who is patient." "I want someone I can count on.") _____

_____

_____

_____

BUILD CONFIDENCE TO DETOXIFY

What can you say to give yourself a pep talk? (Examples: "I deserve healthy relationships." "I choose me." "I don't have to hang out with people who put me down and make me feel bad.") _____

_____

_____

What can you say to the toxic influence to set boundaries? (Examples: "It's not okay for us to do this." "I want our relationship to be healthier and more positive. Here is what is okay for you to do, and what is absolutely not okay.") _____

_____

_____

What can you do and say to reinforce your boundaries and create healthy distance? (Examples: "If you do _____ , I'm going to leave." "When you say _____ , I'm going to take that as a signal that we shouldn't be friends anymore.")

_____

_____

_____

FINAL THOUGHTS

Congratulations for taking a huge step toward feeling better and improving your life! If you've made it this far, it's safe to say you've learned a lot, and you probably have a mess of thoughts swirling in your head. Maybe you're feeling hopeful for the first time in months. Maybe you *want* to feel hopeful, but already the obstacles are stacking up in front of you: You're too busy and there's no time to work on yourself. The people who should be supporting you are actually getting in your way! Or maybe you can't even remember what you just read because your brain is overwhelmed, and your attention is shot.

Don't worry! It's going to be okay, and here's why:

You're already good enough. You're already worthy of love and respect. Right now. As you are. Flaws and all. Try believing in that statement—that you are already good enough, and worthy of love and respect. Say it out loud. "I am already good enough. I am worthy of love and respect." How does that feel? Say it again and keep saying it until it rings true and you start to believe it.

Another thing: There's no rigid timeline for fixing your problems. You literally have the rest of your life. If it seems as if other people are "getting there" faster than you, or have much easier lives, so what? That's their journey. You are on your own journey. It might be a more difficult journey than others have, but it's your very own, and it's as important and meaningful. As long as you keep learning about yourself, and connecting with others, you too will *get there*. And when we say *get there,* we're talking about a real life, one that's important and meaningful for you.

Lastly, healing is not linear. You might make some progress and then slip backward. That's okay. You can always come back to this book later. Getting better is a process and not a final accomplishment. That's really all there is to it: Be kind to yourself, keep learning, and stay connected to good people. We love you and believe in you!

**YOUR FRIENDS AT
MENTAL HEALTH AMERICA**

RESOURCES

MENTAL HEALTH AMERICA

On the Mental Health America website (mhanational.org) you'll find a lot of additional information. Spend some time browsing there to discover the content that's most relevant to you. Here's a sampling:

* **Find a Support Group (mhanational.org/find-support-groups).** This section walks you through various support group options, including a list of specialized resources.
* **Mental Health Screening Tests (mhascreening.org).** Here you'll find quick and easy screening tests for various mental health conditions in order to determine whether you are experiencing symptoms of a particular condition.
* **More Topics (screening.mhanational.org/mental-health-101/).**

Quickly find information here about mental health conditions not covered in this book.

* Where to Get Help (mhanational.org/get-involved/b4stage4-where-get-help-0). This is an interactive questionnaire to guide you through your options for finding therapists and other mental health specialists.

You might also want to follow us on Instagram @mentalhealthamerica, where we share tips and inspiration.

OTHER HELPFUL ORGANIZATIONS

Alcohol and Substance Abuse
Al-Anon (al-anon.org)

Attention Deficit Hyperactivity Disorder
ADHD Attention Deficit Disorder Association (add.org)
Children and Adults with Attention-Deficit/Hyperactivity Disorder (chadd.org)

Autism
Autism Society of America (autismsociety.org)
Autism Spectrum Connection (aspergersyndrome.org):

autism and Asperger's Syndrome support group infor-mation for individuals and family/friends

Bullying

Teens Against Bullying (pacerteensagainstbullying.org): created by teens

Depression and Bipolar Disorder

Depression and Bipolar Support Alliance (dbsalliance.org): peer-based support and resources

Eating Disorders

National Eating Disorders Association (nationaleatingdisorders.org)

General Mental Health

Teen Help (TeenHelp.com): guides on self-esteem, suicide, depression, sexual abuse/trauma, and sub-stance use.

Born This Way Foundation (bornthisway.foundation): kindness programs and partnerships, an active blog, extensive resource list, and crisis hotlines

OK2TALK (ok2talk.org): for sharing personal artistic expressions of recovery, tragedy, struggle, or hope.

Strength of US (strengthofus.org): peer support and resource sharing

Go Ask Alice! (goaskalice.columbia.edu): Q&A focusing on emotional health

National Alliance on Mental Illness (nami.org): family support and advocacy

Grief and Loss

Hospice Foundation of America (hospicefoundation.org): support groups and grief counseling for teens

Homelessness

Covenant House (covenanthouse.org/homeless-shelters): provides housing and supportive services to youth facing homelessness

LGBTQ+

LGBT National Help Center (glbthotline.org or 800-246-7743): provides telephone and e-mail peer counseling as well as information and resources

The Trevor Project (thetrevorproject.org): the largest safe social networking community for LGBTQ youth. The Trevor Lifeline is available 24/7 at 1-866-488-7386.

Physical and Emotional Abuse

Love Is Respect (loveisrespect.org): anonymous and confidential, real-time one-on-one support, information, and advocacy for those involved in dating abuse relationships. Text "LOVEIS" to 22522, or call 1-866-331-9474.

Suicide

American Foundation for Suicide Prevention (afsp.org)

Yellow Ribbon (yellowribbon.org): information and resources about suicide prevention

Tourette Syndrome

Tourette Association of America (tourette.org)

NATIONAL TOLL-FREE HOTLINES

* Boys Town at 1-800-448-3000: crisis, resource, and referral line that assists both teens and parents.

* Child-Help USA at 1-800-422-4453 (1-800-4-A-Child): assists both juvenile and adult survivors of abuse, including sexual abuse. The hotline, staffed by mental health professionals, also provides treatment referrals.

* Covenant House Nineline at 1-800-999-9999: Crisis counselors are available to talk to homeless and at-risk individuals.

* Crisis Text Line: 24-hour support for those in crisis. Text MHA to 741741 from anywhere in the US and within minutes, a live, trained crisis counselor will answer your text. The text exchange is free, confidential, and will not appear on your phone statement.

- ✴ National Domestic Violence Hotline at 1-800-799-SAFE (7233) and 1-800-787-3224 (TTY)
- ✴ National Sexual Assault Telephone Hotline at 1-800-656-HOPE (4673): trained staff members from a sexual assault service provider in your area.
- ✴ National Suicide Prevention Lifeline at 988: 24-hour crisis response.
- ✴ SAMHSA's Treatment Locator at 1-800-662-4357: provides you with information about local mental health services.

FREE MENTAL HEALTH APPS

- ✴ Calm (calm.com): guided meditations, sleep Stories, breathing programs, and relaxing music.
- ✴ Calm Harm (calmharm.co.uk): helps users resist or manage the urge to self-harm.
- ✴ MindShift (anxietycanada.com/resources/mindshift-cbt): designed for young adults with anxiety.
- ✴ NotOK (notokapp.com): developed by teens. In one click, sends a message to trusted contacts with current GPS location. The message reads: "Hey, I'm not OK! Please call, text, or come find me."

* Oak (oakmeditation.com): meditation and breathing app.
* Shine (theshineapp.com): a meditation app started by a Black woman and a half-Japanese woman who didn't see their experiences represented in mainstream wellness programs.
* Ten Percent Happier (tenpercent.com): library of 500+ guided meditations on anxiety, stress, and sleep, as well as videos, bite-sized stories, and inspiration for listening on the go.

30 Ideas for Boosting Your Mental Health

1. **Track gratitude and achievement with a journal.** Include three things you are grateful for and three things you were able to accomplish each day.

2. **Deep breathing.** Sit or lie down comfortably. Rest your hands on your stomach. Slowly count to four while inhaling through your nose. Feel your stomach rise. Hold your breath for a second. Slowly count to four while you exhale, preferably through pursed lips to control the breath. Your stomach will fall slowly. Repeat a few times.

3. **Plan a vacation.** It could be camping with friends or just a drive to someplace new. The act of planning and having something to look forward to can boost your overall happiness for up to eight weeks!

4. **Work your strengths.** Do something you're good at to build self-confidence, then tackle a tougher task.

5. **Keep it cool for a good night's sleep.** The optimal temperature for sleep is between 60 and 67 degrees Fahrenheit.

6. **Mindfulness meditation.** Focus on your breath. Notice without judgment anything that passes through your awareness. If your mind starts to tackle your to-do list, just return to focusing on your breath.

7. **Be creative.** Experiment with a new recipe, write a poem, paint, or try a Pinterest project. Creative expression and overall well-being are linked.

8. **Show some love to someone in your life.** Close, quality relationships are key to happiness and health.

9. **Boost brainpower.** Treat yourself to a couple pieces of dark chocolate every few days. The flavonoids, caffeine, and theobromine in chocolate are thought to work together to improve alertness and mental skills.

10. **Go public—there's power in sharing.** If you have personal experience with mental illness or recovery, share on Twitter, Instagram, and Tumblr with #mentalillnessfeelslike. Check out what other people are saying at mhanational.org/mentalillnessfeelslike.

11. **Feeling anxious?** Do some coloring for about twenty minutes to help you clear your mind. Pick a design that's geometric and a little complicated for the best effect. Search online for printable coloring pages; there are hundreds available.

12. **Take time to laugh.** Hang out with a fun friend, watch a comedy, or check out goofy videos online. Laughter helps reduce anxiety.

13. **Go off the grid.** Leave your smart phone at home for a day and disconnect from constant emails, alerts, and other interruptions. Spend time doing something fun with someone face-to-face.

14. **Dance around while you do chores or clean your room.** Dancing reduces levels of cortisol (the stress hormone) and increases endorphins (the body's "feel-good" chemical).

15. **Go ahead and yawn.** Studies suggest that yawning helps cool the brain and improves alertness and mental efficiency.

16. **Relax in a warm bath once a week.** Try adding Epsom salts to soothe and help boost magnesium levels, which can be depleted by stress.

17. **Do your best to take in fifteen minutes of sunshine.** Sunlight synthesizes vitamin D, which experts believe is a mood elevator.

18. **Repeat a mantra.** Sit quietly and pick any meaningful or soothing word, phrase, or sound, such as "May I be calm," "I am okay," or "Peace." You can repeat the mantra aloud or silently. Experts say the repetition creates a physical relaxation response.

19. **Write it all down.** Has something been bothering you? Let it all out . . . on paper. Writing about upsetting experiences can reduce symptoms of depression.

20. **Spend some time with a furry friend.** Time with animals lowers the stress hormone cortisol, and boosts oxytocin, which stimulates feelings of happiness. If you don't have a pet, hang out with a friend who does, or volunteer at a shelter.

21. **Visualization.** Close your eyes, relax, and imagine a peaceful place, like a forest. Engage your senses: Hear the crunching leaves, smell the damp soil, feel the breeze.

22. **Be a tourist in your own town.** Often people only explore attractions on trips, but you may be surprised what cool things are in your own backyard.

23. **Try prepping your lunches or picking out your clothes for the next week.** You'll save some time in the mornings and have a sense of control about the week ahead.

24. **Work some omega-3 fatty acids into your diet:** foods like wild salmon, flaxseed, and walnuts. They are linked to decreased rates of depression and schizophrenia among their many benefits. Fish oil supplements work, but eating your omega-3s in foods also helps build health gut bacteria.

25. **Practice forgiveness**—even if it's just forgiving that person who cut you off on the way into school. People who forgive have better mental health and report being more satisfied with their lives.

26. **Participate in a meditative form of exercise.** Try tai chi or qigong, which use soothing, flowing motions.

27. **Smile when you feel stressed.** It may not be the easiest thing to do, but smiling can help lower your heart rate and calm you down.

28. **Send a thank-you note**—not for a material item, but to let someone know why you appreciate them. Written expressions of gratitude are linked to increased happiness.

29. **Do something with friends and family:** Have a cookout, go to a park, or play a game. People are twelve times more likely to feel happy on days that they spend six hours with friends and family.

30. **Take thirty minutes to go for a walk in nature.** It can be a stroll through a park or a hike in the woods. Research shows that being in nature can increase energy levels, reduce depression, and boost well-being.

Further Reading

Are u ok?: A Guide to Caring for Your Mental Health
by Kati Morton (Da Capo, 2018)

(Don't) Call Me Crazy
edited by Kelly Jensen (Algonquin, 2018)

It's All Absolutely Fine: Life Is Complicated So I've Drawn It Instead
by Ruby Elliot (Andrews McMeel, 2017)

Just As You Are: A Teen's Guide to Self-Acceptance and Lasting Self-Esteem
by Michelle Skeen and Kelly Skeen (Instant Help, 2018)

Mindfulness and Meditation: Handling Life with a Calm and Focused Mind
by Whitney Stewart (Twenty-First Century Books, 2019)

Mind Your Head
by Juno Dawson (Hot Key Books, 2016)

Your Brain Needs a Hug: Life, Love, Mental Health, and Sandwiches by Rae Earl (Imprint, 2019)